A TIME OF LEGENDS

Chronicles of *the* Yellowstone Wolves

RICK McINTYRE AND DAVID A. POULSEN

A TIME OF LEGENDS

The Story of Two Fearless Wolves—and One Rebel

GREYSTONE KIDS

GREYSTONE BOOKS • VANCOUVER/BERKELEY/LONDON

*For the founding wolves of Yellowstone's
Wolf Reintroduction Project*

RM

*For John and Marilyn Dekok, Chris Martens,
and Pia Sorensen—good friends, great neighbors*
and
*Stephanie Gregorwich and Jenn Plamondon
at the Young Alberta Book Society, for their
tremendous work in bringing literary artists
into classrooms throughout the province*

DAP

Contents

The Packs . . . 2
A Lifetime of Studying Wolves . . . 5
Previously, in the Chronicles
of the Yellowstone Wolves . . . 7

**PART ONE: A Royal Pair—
The Reign of 21 and 42**

1. A Druid Spring . . . 15
2. The Wars . . . 25
3. An Incredible Journey and a New Arrival . . . 35
4. A Good Druid Year . . . 43
5. Two Farewells . . . 51

PART TWO: The Rise of 302

6. A New Beginning . . . 63
7. A Druid Resurgence . . . 73
8. The Times, They Are a-Changin' . . . 87
9. The New and Improved 302 . . . 99
10. The Blacktail Pack . . . 107

About the Authors . . . 122

The Packs

FEMALE   MALE

These family trees show you how the wolves you're reading about in this series are related to each other. In the family trees, male wolves are shown in black and females in gray.

Crystal Creek Pack

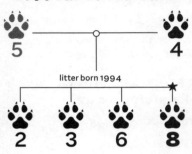

This pack, originally from Alberta, Canada, was released into Yellowstone in January 1995 as part of the Wolf Reintroduction Program. **Wolf 8's** story is told in *The Unlikely Hero*.

Rose Creek Pack

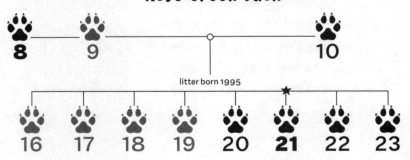

When Wolf 10 was illegally shot and killed, Wolf 8 formed a bond with Wolf 9. He became the Rose Creek alpha male, and the adoptive father to 9's pups. The story of his relationship with **Wolf 21** is told in *The Unlikely Hero*.

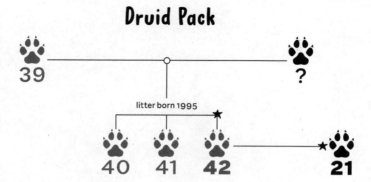

The relationship between **Wolves 42 and 21** was special—a pairing that led to the birth of many pups and had a lasting impact on the wolf population in Yellowstone. To learn more, keep reading!

Wolf 302—the mischief-making rebel you're about to meet—had a former Crystal Creek wolf as his father and former Rose Creek female as his mother. Because wolf family trees are complicated, that meant 302 was a nephew to both 21 and 8!

A lifetime of Studying Wolves

Rick McIntyre has devoted his life to the study of wolves. For more than two decades, he was part of the team of biologists, rangers, and park staff who studied the wolf population in Yellowstone after the wolves were reintroduced in 1995, and he continues to study and write about the wolves today. Rick grew up in a rural part of Massachusetts, and as a boy roamed the nearby woods and fields to be with and observe the animals he had already come to love. The more time Rick spent outdoors, the more he became interested in the wildlife he saw around him.

Rick studied forestry at the University of Massachusetts and, after graduating, continued to study the animals of the national parks in which he worked. But always Rick's greatest interest was wolves. As he came to know more about these amazing animals, he realized that wolves are the closest of all of nature's creatures to humans, particularly in the way they interact with and care for the members of their family.

A Time of Legends

After many years of watching wolves and studying their behavior in Yellowstone, Rick put his writing talents to work. He created a series of books designed to tell the world the stories of the Yellowstone wolves, including Wolf 8, Wolf 21, Wolf 42, and Wolf 302—four of the most famous wolves ever. Now Rick and award-winning Canadian author David A. Poulsen have teamed up to retell those stories for younger readers. The first of the books in the Chronicles of the Yellowstone Wolves series was *The Unlikely Hero: The Story of Wolf 8*. In this, the second book, the story continues...

Previously, in the Chronicles of the Yellowstone Wolves...

Wolf 21 was resting.

There wasn't really much time for resting—not with six adult wolves and twenty-one pups that needed a protector and provider. As the alpha male of the Druid wolf pack, 21 was that leader and that father.

But for now, he was getting some downtime. He was lying on a knoll and watching several of his pups, both male and female, playing in a pleasant open meadow. They were having fun chasing one another, wrestling, playing tug-of-war with sticks, and competing in another of their favorite games: king of the mountain. One of the pups would stand atop a rise in the meadow and fight off the other pups until, eventually, one would succeed in knocking the "king" off their perch and taking over for a while.

21 thought about joining in the fun. There wasn't an adult wolf in all of Yellowstone National Park that loved

A Time of Legends

playing more than 21. And he would like nothing better than a good romp with his family. But 21 also knew that the responsibilities of protecting and providing food for this large group of pups was a tiring and seemingly endless job.

So instead of giving in to the temptation of racing down the hill and leaping into the middle of their play, he stayed where he was. For a little while, not long, 21— the great alpha male of the Druid pack—slept.

◇ ◇ ◇

Life hadn't been easy for 21. His mother and father, Wolves 9 and 10, had been part of the 1995 Wolf Reintroduction Project that brought fourteen wolves, some adults and some pups, to Yellowstone National Park. They were the first wolves in Yellowstone since 1926, when the American government had ordered the elimination of the last surviving wolves in the park.

Wolves 9 and 10 were the alpha pair of the Rose Creek pack. Not long after they were released from the acclimation pen where they'd been kept when they were first brought to Yellowstone, Wolf 9 gave birth to eight pups. 21 was one of those pups. Tragically, on the day the pups were born, their father, Wolf 10, was illegally shot and killed. (The man who did that was sent to prison for his crime.)

That meant Wolf 9 would have to raise her pups all by herself, an almost impossible task. To give the

Previously, in the Chronicles of the Yellowstone Wolves...

one-parent family at least a fighting chance at survival, park staff recaptured Wolf 9 and the pups and returned them to the acclimation pen. With the humans bringing food to the enclosure, at least 9 wouldn't have to leave her pups alone in the forest while she hunted for food to feed them.

Wolf 8 was one of the founding members of the wolf reintroduction, coming to Yellowstone as a pup. In fact, he was the smallest of a litter of four, and was constantly picked on and bullied by his three brothers. Despite his difficult beginnings, Wolf 8 quickly showed his independent spirit. During one of his solitary rambles through the park he encountered first Wolf 9's pups (they quickly became friends) and then 9 herself. Though still very young, 8 became the mate to Wolf 9 and the adopted father to those pups. Almost immediately, he proved himself a worthy mate and father, and would go on to become one of the greatest alpha males to ever live in Yellowstone.

But even great wolves have their share of challenges. As the Wolf Reintroduction Project expanded, bringing new packs to the park, 8 faced competition. One spring day, not long after 8 and 9 had their first pups together, 8 spotted one of the new packs—the Druids—charging down a hill toward him and his family. In the lead was the huge and tremendously strong Wolf 38. 8 didn't hesitate: though he was much smaller than 38, he ran straight at the marauders who posed such a terrible threat to his family and launched himself at 38. A dramatic fight ensued, and when it was over, Wolf 8 was the victor. But instead of killing his defeated rival, as is often the case when wolves fight, 8 banished 38 and chased him off to make sure the Druid alpha male wouldn't even think about coming back.

It was an amazing moment. The underdog not only successfully defended his family against all odds but chose to show mercy to his opponent. Courage and compassion were qualities that 8 would show over and over. And 21, a yearling at the time of the battle, watched his adoptive father as it all unfolded. 21 was with 8 for two and a half years, and during that time was taught the lessons that would prepare him for when he became an adult wolf: how to hunt, how to raise pups, and how to fulfill an alpha male's responsibilities to his family.

Eventually the time came for 21 to leave his family and strike out on his own. Attracted by howling and the scent of one particular female, Wolf 42, 21 joined the rival Druid pack after the death of 38 and raised 38's pups, just as 8 had done for 21 and his brothers and sisters.

21 faced a major challenge when he joined the Druids. That challenge was Wolf 40—a vicious and cruel female who was sister to 42. 40 had driven her mother and one of her sisters out of the pack, and twice killed 42's pups. Although her viciousness toward 42 continued,

Previously, in the Chronicles of the Yellowstone Wolves...

21 seemed to have a rule that he would never harm a female wolf—even one as mean and violent as 40. For a time he tried to win her over, bringing her into playtimes with the pups and standing between her and 42 when 40 tried to attack and abuse her much more gentle sister.

But all of that changed in the spring of 2000, when 40 once again prepared to attack 42's pups. This time, 42 was ready to stand up to her sister and fight for the lives of her pups. But she'd need help to win this battle. When 40 took the upper hand in the fight, two younger mothers, who had also experienced 40's terrible temper and had always been treated with kindness by 42, came to the aid of their friend. Together, the three females overpowered 40. She suffered serious injuries and died soon after.

With Wolf 40 out of the picture, 42 became the pack's alpha female. Her compassion was evident as she quickly took over the care and feeding of 40's pups, a big job on top of looking after her own litter. Almost overnight the personality of the Druid pack changed. The kind but capable leadership of 42, coupled with 21's ability to protect and provide food for the Druid family, transformed the pack that had once been known as the "bad wolves of Lamar" into one of Yellowstone's most loved and admired.

◇ ◇ ◇

A Time of Legends

Up on the knoll, 21's short but restful nap was over. It was now time to return to the den area where the rest of the Druids were gathered...

Late one day, I watched 21, the setting sun behind him. His shadow projected 50 feet (15 meters) toward me. The image struck me as symbolic of the impact he was having on Yellowstone and the people who knew him. I had begun to think we'd entered a golden age for wolves in the park. It was a time of legends, a time when giants strode the land. It was the time of Wolves 21 and 42. ★ RICK

PART ONE

A Royal Pair—
The Reign of 21 and 42

Wolves 21 (right) and 42 (left)

1

A Druid Spring

It was late in the spring of 2000. The elk that were the main source of food for the Yellowstone wolves were giving birth to their calves at just about the same time that wolf pups were switching from mother's milk to eating meat.

On one particularly warm June afternoon with the sky a hazy blue, the Druids were hunting. One of the young females, Wolf 106, spotted an elk cow and moved toward her. The cow chased her away, but 106 stayed close, circling and sniffing the area where the elk cow had been. 21 and 42 soon joined her in the search. Suddenly, 106 raced forward, her head down. She had found the elk cow's calf.

The alphas raced in and carried off the calf. When they had run for a time, they set down the dead calf and began to feed. After a moment, 21 hesitated and then stepped back, watching as the two females continued to enjoy their meal. Finally, he turned and walked away.

He was hungry after a long hunt, but he wanted the females to have that calf to themselves. He had unselfishly passed up a meal to let the two nursing mothers eat, an example of the leadership 21 had displayed over and over again.

It had been a busy spring and would continue to be that way, with six adults and twenty-one pups now making up the Druid pack. Keeping that many pups fed, cared for, and safe would be a huge challenge for the pack's adults, in particular the alphas 21 and 42. The last two years had seen poor pup survival rates among the Druids, mostly because of the lack of leadership and the murderous jealousy demonstrated by Wolf 40 when she was the alpha female.

And though 42 was a very different wolf from her sister, it wouldn't be an easy summer for the Druids. In the world wolves inhabit, even when things seem relatively quiet, there are almost daily challenges and threats. One lazy July day, the Druid family was resting through the hottest part of the afternoon. Without warning, a massive grizzly approached the den area, heading directly for some of the pups that were sprawled in the shade of a few large spruce trees. 21 immediately charged the intruder and bit it. He knew it was a dangerous move, even for a wolf as strong and quick as he was. A single bite or swipe from one of the bear's enormous paws could end a wolf's life, but 21 was fearless when it came to protecting his family. Relying on his speed and elusiveness to keep himself safe, he retreated and then leaped forward to bite the massive beast again. And again.

The bear finally backed off, but it remained in the area. He had probably been hoping to steal an elk carcass from the wolves. Fortunately for the Druids, the bear showed no further interest in the pups, no doubt reluctant to face the valiant—and quite irritating!—leader of this pack anymore that day. At last the bear slunk off, hoping to find a meal that wasn't quite as much work and aggravation. 21 had again displayed the courage and leadership that were required of a pack's alpha male, whose first job was to protect the other members of the pack. It was a job 21 did very well.

Things might have gone differently if the bear had lumbered by the following day—when the Druids brought down a big bull elk in the same area. The pups, now three months old, gathered round to feed on the carcass. It was the first time this year's litter had eaten at a fresh kill, and one pup tore off a slab of meat and buried it, apparently planning for a future meal. Over the next few days, 21 fed at this carcass and another kill, and then returned to the den area to regurgitate food for the pups. Then he'd repeat the process, leaving almost immediately to get more meat for the youngest members of the pack.

The never-ending work of keeping four litters of hungry pups fed was taking a toll on the alpha male. Even though he was exhausted, he still pushed himself to provide the nourishment the pups required. But even a wolf with 21's stamina will eventually give in to the need for rest.

A few days later, when the pups were pestering him to play, he ran down a hill, crossed a nearby road, and settled into a thick clump of willows to escape the endlessly persistent pups. 21 was desperate for a little sleep. It turned out to be *very* little sleep—about a half hour is all—but when he returned to the pups, 21 was at least somewhat refreshed and ready to tackle whatever the next leadership challenge might be.

On August 15 help arrived. A stranger appeared on the scene—a gray male who hadn't been seen in Druid territory before. 21 welcomed the new arrival, who turned out to be a nephew, born to 21's sister, who was now the alpha female of the Rose Creek pack. The nephew became known as New Gray. He immediately went to work helping with the feeding, regurgitating meat for several pups. And when another grizzly intruded upon the Druid site it was New Gray who swung into action. He charged the bear and, with 21 and 42 looking on approvingly, drove it off. The newcomer was quickly proving to be a valuable addition, and his presence allowed 21 and 42 to get more rest than they had in quite a while.

Summer moved into fall, and the pups got bigger and stronger, which meant less stress and a bit less work for 21 and 42. Now that they were more relaxed, they finally had the time to be more affectionate with one another. 21 would often lick 42's face and wag his tail at her. She would often respond with teasing feints, and they'd gently wrestle. The pair had known each other for three years now, but for much of that time they'd had to contend with the very unpleasant Wolf 40. Now, at last, they were able to enjoy each other's company like they had when they first met. Romeo and Juliet were once again able to act like Romeo and Juliet.

With the arrival of winter, the pups were more capable of participating in the all-important hunts. Winter snow is actually an advantage for wolves. When wolves run on snow, their big paws spread out, creating a snowshoe effect that keeps them on or near the surface of the snow and allows them to cover more ground more quickly. As well, wolves will travel in single file, with the lead wolf breaking trail and the rest of the pack following behind. The wolves will trade off in the lead position so that one wolf doesn't have to do all the exhausting work of making a trail. Often, the older wolves will be at the back of the line, leaving the trail-breaking to the younger members of the pack.

The single-file strategy worked to perfection in late December as the Druids pursued a cow elk across snow-covered terrain. The lead yearling was able to get hold of the elk's hind leg to slow her down. A black pup, just eight months old, ran past the elk and got hold of her neck. The rest of the pack then surrounded the cow, and together they brought her down.

> As the year ended, I thought about what a tremendous accomplishment the Druid adults had achieved with pup survival. Twenty of the twenty-one pups made it to the new year, a 95 percent survival rate, compared to 33 percent the previous year. There was one major difference between those two years: with her kind and non-aggressive personality—so different from Wolf 40—42 seemed to be able to get all the wolves to cooperate and work together. ★ RICK

◇ ◇ ◇

By the end of February 2001, the breeding season—the time when male and female wolves mate and create the pups that will be born later in the spring—was over for another year. In just eight weeks, the new pups would be born as the cycle of life continued for the Yellowstone wolves. While there had been a little animosity in the pack (21 found himself having to protect 42 from the romantic inclinations of New Gray), harmony was still very much in evidence among the Druid wolves. The bond between 21 and 42 was as strong as ever. Face-licking, playful romping, and gentle playfighting were the outward signs of their feelings for one another. Theirs was a unique love story, and that love grew stronger with each passing year. As the time for 42 to have her litter of pups drew nearer, 21 continued to show his tremendous affection both for his mate and the younger wolves.

While she seemed more than willing to return her mate's affection, 42 was also busy preparing the den that would be home for her and her soon-to-arrive pups. The spot she had chosen was the traditional Druid site that had been the favored den of her sister, Wolf 40, when she was alive. 42 was also busy keeping peace and harmony in the Druid family. Wolf 106 had always been the lowest-ranking of the three sisters that were part of the Druid adult group, but that was about to change. One day, 106 approached Wolf 103, her sister, and was very aggressive, pinning her sibling to the ground and standing over her, clearly displaying her superiority. She repeated that action several times over the next few days. When the unpleasant behavior continued, 42 intervened. She would either pin 106 or distract her to allow 103 to run to safety. It was part of the ongoing air of cooperation and peaceful coexistence 42 worked to foster, in part to ensure that the females worked together when the pups were born.

One of the three young sisters, Wolf 105, had denned about 10 miles (16 kilometers) to the west of the main

Druid den and Wolf 42, and both mothers had their pups around the same time. 21 was kept especially busy going on hunts and bringing food to both of the females, since neither could leave their pups to hunt or even feed from another wolf's kill.

42's choice of denning site was wise. She had lived in the valley for most of her five years, and she knew the area around that den was a favorite spot for elk cows to give birth to their calves. The young Druid mother didn't have 42's experience. She'd established her den in an area where there were not any elk in the spring, when pups need a lot of food. Even with 21 trying to help, her litter was in danger. Eventually, 105 carried her surviving pups one by one to 42's den—a decision that saved their lives.

Wolves are excellent hunters and are especially adept at hunting elk, which make up a large percentage of their diet. In fact, as spring stretched into summer, the Druids brought down several of the animals. The Druid adults and yearlings worked well together and got a big bull right near 42's denning area. But the wolves' hunting expertise failed them later that same day when they met up with a very different and much smaller animal—a beaver.

The Druids encountered this particular beaver during a casual stroll upriver from their main den. The beaver spotted the wolves at about the same time the

A Druid Spring

wolves spotted it. The beaver made a loud tail slap, warning its family that there were predators in the area. 42 and five other wolves waded back and forth in the river near the beaver's lodge, searching for the elusive rodent, with no luck. At one point, 21 leaped into the water to join in the search while several other Druids watched from the bank. A gray yearling worked his way to a spot near the lodge, turned, and found himself face-to-face with the beaver. The beaver weighed in at 50 to 60 pounds (23 to 27 kilograms)—a good-sized rodent to be sure. It swam closer to the wolf and slapped its tail on the water once again. The young wolf took off with *his* tail tucked between his legs. Over the next two hours the beaver—which seemed well equipped to take care of itself in the presence of wolves—made thirty-nine alarm splashes. The wolves never did get that beaver, but 21 seemed to enjoy the encounter. It was good training for the yearlings, and it provided an afternoon of fun for the adult wolves.

By late summer of 2001, the Druid pack numbered thirty-seven—with twenty-six adults and eleven pups from the spring's litters surviving. It was a world-record for any known wolf pack, and it still stands today.

September 11, 2001, started off just like any other morning. I happened to have my car radio on and heard the news of the terrorist attack on the World Trade Center

A Time of Legends

in New York City. That terrible day is often referred to as 9/11—a numeric reference to the month and date the attacks took place. Years later, a Yellowstone male wolf was collared and assigned the number 911. When he was an old wolf, 911 died in an extraordinarily heroic manner, an act that reminded me of the courageous firefighters, police officers, medical personnel, and other people who tried to help victims of the attack and lost their lives in the process. ★ RICK

The Wars

On October 19 of that same year, just a couple of months after the humorous and unsuccessful beaver encounter, a much more serious event took place. Druid territory was invaded. On the western side of the park, about 25 miles (40 kilometers) from Lamar Valley, the Nez Perce pack roamed. Every wolf in that pack was gray, while the Druids were mostly black.

There were eighteen adults in the Nez Perce group—fewer than the twenty-six adults in the Druid pack. That should have meant an advantage for the pack led by 21 and his mate, 42, but the Druids were not always together. And that was exactly the case on that fall morning. 21 and six other Druids were in one part of Lamar Valley, while 42 and another ten pack members had been bedded down 2 miles (3 kilometers) away. 42 was leading her group east toward 21 and company when a cluster of the Nez Perce pack burst out of the woods, on the attack.

It took only a moment for 42 to step away from the unfolding battle and howl a plea for help. 21 and his group howled back and immediately raced off in 42's direction. Not surprisingly given his alpha male status, 21 was out in front of the band of rescuers. As he got closer to 42 and the other wolves, he jumped up on his hind legs to get a better look at what was going on. 42, who had blood on her hip from an encounter with one of the attacking wolves, was leading her group toward 21. The Nez Perce marauders saw them coming, and they retreated to the woods to try to avoid facing the reinforcements. When 21 reached 42, he sniffed her wound, trying to learn more about what had happened. Straight away, he picked up the scent of the Nez Perce invaders.

Had the Nez Perce wolves stayed in the woods, the battle might have ended there. But it was then that the invaders made a mistake. Eight of their number charged out of the woods in pursuit of several young Druids. Instantly, 21 swung into action. He took the lead and, with fifteen Druids right behind him, charged straight at the Nez Perce wolves, who fled into the trees once again. 21 didn't look back to see if the other Druid pack members were with him. He didn't care. He roared directly into the gang of Nez Perce wolves—more than willing to fight them by himself if that's what it took.

The Wars

I will never forget that moment when 21, out in front of the other Druids, ran straight into the cluster of eight Nez Perce wolves. It was a stunning display of courage in the middle of a battle. That image of a father wolf risking his life to protect his mate and family forever defined the character of 21 for me. ★ RICK

The Nez Perce wolves wanted no part of the enraged 21. They fled in every direction, eventually disappearing to the southwest. 21 and 42 prowled the woods, looking for signs of the intruders. Soon they were joined by other Druids, who helped conduct a sweep of the area in search of any members from the enemy party. 21 was taking no chances. He wanted to be sure that 42 and the other Druids were no longer in danger—and he was incensed that his mate had been attacked and injured by the trespassing wolves.

Wolf 21 may have been looking for revenge, but this battle was over. After initiating their brazen attack, the Nez Perce wolves had clearly lost their nerve and beat a hasty retreat out of Druid territory. The Druids may have held their ground, but they didn't escape completely unharmed. A black yearling male suffered an injured leg in the fight and by the next morning was having trouble getting around. Even lying down was difficult. The Druids left the area, but 21 returned later and brought food to the injured yearling, who he had sired with Wolf 105. When the main pack returned a few days later, the yearling—who would later be given

A Time of Legends

the number 253—was able to move around with them for short distances, though he held his injured leg in the air, not allowing his paw to touch the ground. Two days later, a number of the Druids returned from feeding at a fresh elk kill. One of the pups was carrying a leg from the carcass. He dropped the leg in front of his older brother, 253. A pup that had, until recently, had food brought to him was now bringing meat to an incapacitated older brother—a sign of selflessness and maturity.

As for Wolf 253, he had quite a story to tell. He was one of the pups that had been saved when the villainous Wolf 40 had tried, not for the first time, to kill all the pups that weren't hers. His mother, Wolf 105, was one of the females who had joined 42 in standing up to Wolf 40 and inflicting the injuries that would finally claim her life. A wolf that almost didn't survive his earliest days had now suffered a serious injury in a fight with a rival wolf pack, an injury that would become a permanent disability. But his story was a long way from over. In fact, he would eventually be part of one of the most remarkable journeys ever undertaken by a wolf (see the next chapter for more about that!).

In November, just weeks after the battle with the Nez Perce pack, the Druids began a series of round trips to a part of their home territory called Hellroaring Creek. During one of those trips back and forth—a round-trip distance of 40 miles (64 kilometers)—the Druids were lying down, taking a break. 21 had found an elk leg bone and was chewing on it when one of the pups came over to him, wanting to play. Always willing to join his sons and daughters in their games, 21 looked up from the elk leg. The pup gently hit his father on the head with a paw. 21 did a playful air-snap at the pup, who then lay on the ground and gently batted 21 with both paws. A raven came by at just that moment, and 21 turned to chase it. The pup, seeing an opportunity, grabbed the bone his father had been enjoying and raced off. 21 let the pup get way with the theft. Just a short distance away, 253, the injured yearling, was also playing with one of the pups. He still couldn't put weight on his injured leg, but he was clearly feeling at least a little better.

Later that month, the Druids were on the move. 253 was in the lead, still using just three legs. For a time, 21 advanced to head up the pack. Soon enough, 253 passed him and was again the lead wolf. He might never again use his injured leg properly, but he wasn't about to let that keep him from participating fully in the pack's activities. In this way, he was displaying the courage and stamina that were also such an important part of his father's personality.

But 21 had demonstrated more than just toughness to his pack. Concern for others had always been on display in his interactions with his family. That winter, when several of the young Druids teamed up to kill a cow elk, one of the yearlings, Wolf 224, played a major role in making that hunt a success, grabbing hold of the elk's hind leg and refusing to let go, even as she attempted to kick back at him. After the elk was down, the other young wolves ganged up on 224 and picked on him, driving him away from the carcass. 21 saw what was happening and went to where 224 had bedded down. The young wolf licked his father on the face. 21 returned the gesture and then went to the carcass as 224 followed along. With 21 standing by him, the yearling finally got to eat without any of the other wolves bothering him.

> **Because of his size and fighting ability, 21 had probably never been picked on, but I think he had empathy for the bullied yearling. It seemed as if he could imagine how the younger wolf felt. That incident, and the one where he came back to check on the injured 253 and brought him food, showed how 21 watched over the younger wolves in the pack and gave special attention to those that were having a hard time—just like a human father would to a son or daughter. ★ RICK**

◇ ◇ ◇

The arrival of 2002 marked a significant change in the Druid pack. A number of young female Druids were ready to link up with males from other packs and form new ones with their chosen mates. The result was a decrease in the size of the Druid pack, which had been, for a time, a huge group. While this splintering off was a completely natural occurrence, the departure of a number of the younger wolves meant the Druids would no longer be the dominant force they had been for so long. Still, Druid females were part of the formation of three new packs: the Agate, Buffalo Fork, and Geode packs. That meant that while the Druid pack itself may have been shrinking in size, the importance of 21's sons and daughters was beginning to dominate the Yellowstone area.

The evening of March 13 was pleasant. A soft wind was blowing out of the west and the temperature was tolerable for that early in the spring. 21, 42, and one black pup were near the bottom of a hill in the Hellroaring Creek area that had, in recent years, become a second home to the Druids. They spotted six wolves from the Geode pack higher up the hill and coming their way. The newly formed Geode pack—which included former Druid female Wolf 106—were clearly set on taking over the Hellroaring territory as their own.

The three Druids howled, in part a warning to the invaders and in part an expression of outrage. The six Geodes group-howled in response, a warning of their own and a statement of claim to the area. They then began to charge downhill at 21, 42, and the black pup.

21 immediately raced up the hill and straight at the oncoming Geodes, who were confident that their larger number would mean easy victory.

But 21 had other ideas. He had been outnumbered before, and having only 42 and one young pup as backup did not worry him at all. He sped up as they closed in on the Geodes.

Intimidated by the boldness of this big and obviously tough alpha male, the Geodes scattered. 21 first chased a black wolf, and then charged at the Geode alpha male, a big gray. A large black male pursued 42, who dodged him and then fought back. 21 raced to her side and together they ran off her attacker. Then 21 turned his attention back to the alpha male, pinning him and repeatedly biting the big gray as he squirmed on the ground.

Eventually, 21 let the alpha go, but he was back soon enough with another wolf. Now two big males teamed up and chased 21, who ran a short distance and then turned to face the challengers. When the Geode alpha male fled in panic, 21 was right on his tail, biting him on the back as he tried to escape. Eventually, 21 let him go and ran back to check on 42. The Geode alpha male was back and standing shoulder to shoulder with the alpha female, Wolf 106. 21 first pursued the big black Geode male and then turned his attention, once again, to the alpha pair—until all three ran from his relentless attacks.

For a few moments the wolves disappeared into the adjacent woods. But the battle wasn't over. When the Geodes reappeared, 21 and 42 once again found themselves surrounded. Before the Geodes could mount a coordinated attack, 21 swung into action and again charged directly at them. First, the Geodes scattered, and then the six exhausted wolves came together to think about their next move.

The black Druid pup, not really understanding the fight for territory that was taking place around him, had joined up with the Geodes, enjoying a reunion with 106—a female he knew very well from her time as a Druid. Problem was, the rest of the Geodes weren't all that welcoming to the pup, who they saw as an enemy. They ran at the younger black, who took off downhill toward 21. The big gray alpha was leading the charge, and when he got to 21, they fought again. When the other Geodes arrived to help their male leader, 21 ran off with the pup beside him, trying to protect the younger wolf. The Geodes chased the pair into woods and attacked 21. The move allowed the black pup to escape, but it put 21 in grave danger. All six Geodes were now attacking 21, biting him at will. It seemed like this might be the end of the mighty 21.

Suddenly, the Geodes turned and ran away. 42 and 253 were charging up the hill, along with several other Druids who had not yet been a part of the fight but had seen what was happening to 21. Together, they made their way to where 21 was standing his ground. Seeing them coming hard had taken the fight out of the Geodes—they couldn't get away fast enough.

After making sure the Geodes were well and truly gone, 42 returned to check on her mate. He had a bloodied hip but other than that seemed to be in relatively good health. The warrior who had so often risked his life to fight for his family and his pack had been repaid in kind. This time, the combined courage and strength of the pack had saved his life.

The next day, 21 and 42 set out for the Druids' traditional den area. For a while, 21 led, well ahead of 42, who moving more slowly as she was well into a pregnancy. Realizing his mate had fallen back, 21 lay down and waited for her to catch up. When she passed him, 21 got up and followed her.

> **On that day, I thought about all the times I had seen 21 follow 42's lead. The Druids often ignored 21 when he wanted to go in a particular direction, but they would follow 42 when she led. That was one of the clear illustrations that 42 was the real leader of the pack, not 21. I think he understood that and had no problem with her being in charge. ★ RICK**

An Incredible Journey and a New Arrival

It was late October 2002 when Wolf 253 decided to strike out on his own. One day, he was leading his family to the Chalcedony Creek rendezvous site, where the growing pups could safely explore and play. The next day, he was gone.

Although he was the beta (second-ranking) male in the Druid pack and would have succeeded 21 as the alpha, the desire to leave, find a mate, and start his own pack was strong. His decision, however, came with risks. Although 253 had shown himself to be a tough and capable leader like his father, his injured leg meant that, as a lone wolf, he'd have little chance of survival if challenged by a rival pack. And yet he set out on his journey—walking away from the pack and disappearing into the dense forest.

None of the Druids had any idea what had happened to the wolf that had been a such an important part of

A Time of Legends

their pack for so long. Days went by, and then days stretched into weeks. Still no sign of 253. He didn't return to the Druids, but he hadn't shown up as a member of any of the rival packs in the area, either.

On the last day of November, a coyote trapper in the Wasatch Mountains, 25 miles (40 kilometers) northeast of Salt Lake City, went out to check his traps and found a large black wolf in one, held by the right front leg. The trapper saw a second set of wolf tracks, a sign that the captured wolf, a male, had been traveling with a companion, probably a female. The man tied the wolf's legs together, freed him from the trap, and drove him to the local Utah Department of Natural Resources warden, who put the wolf in a kennel and then fed and watered him.

That wolf was 253—the first confirmed wolf in Utah in over seventy years. And the place where he was found was about 200 miles (320 kilometers) from Lamar Valley.

> **Wolf 253 was released near the south entrance to Yellowstone on December 2, still 60 miles (97 kilometers) from Lamar Valley. I picked up his radio collar signal in Lamar Valley on December 20, sixty-five days after I had last seen him with the Druids. And days later, he was back with his family. ★ RICK**

The story of the courage and stamina of Wolf 253 soon made him a national celebrity. An article in the

An Incredible Journey and a New Arrival

Salt Lake Tribune read "Beloved Wolf, 253, Running With Original Pack." He left the Druid pack with one bad leg and made the return trip to his home in Lamar Valley on two bad legs. For a while, whenever the pack stopped to rest, 253 would lie down and lick his sore front paw. 21 would often bed down next to him, an indication that 21, as he so often had, was offering support and encouragement to a fellow pack member, this time his son.

But it wasn't long before 253 was able to keep up to the rest of the Druids, even when 21 was setting a rapid pace. And soon after that he was back to being a contributing member of the pack, tending pups, hunting elk, and defending the pack's den from unwelcome visitors—bears and other would-be predators.

It is a remarkable story of another of 21's offspring who had clearly inherited many of his noble father's finest traits.

◇ ◇ ◇

On January 17, 2003, another male began what was to be a long association with the Druid pack. However, this wolf was not nearly as welcome as the returning 253. It was early morning and bitterly cold. The Druids were gathered east of their den, howling and looking to the southwest. A lone wolf was standing not far away, eyes fixed on the pack. He was young, big, and had a sleek, black coat. He was a very good-looking fellow. If wolves had movie stars in their world, this newcomer would be the next big thing.

> That new male on the scene was later captured, collared, and given the number 302. Genetic testing determined he was born in 2000, which made him two years and eight months old. His mother was 21's half-sister, which meant that 302 was 21's nephew. Even though the two wolves were closely related, they were total opposites in personality, as I would soon learn. ★ RICK

The wolf mating season was about to start, and it was quite obvious what the handsome stranger had in mind. At that time, there were three young adult (teenagers in human years) females in the Druid pack: Wolf 255 and two wolves who sported names based on the markings on their coats: U Black and Half Black. It seemed that the intruder's plan was to lure the young females away from the Druids and start his own pack.

21 had different ideas. He glared unhappily at the newcomer and then led the Druids into a nearby forest. It wasn't long before Half Black came out of the trees and approached this cool new stranger, her tail wagging a warm welcome. But instead of returning the obviously smitten young female's pleasant greeting, 302 turned and ran off, his tail tucked between his legs—no doubt because he saw what was happening just *behind* Half Black. 21 and 42 had come charging out of the wooded

area, and it was clear they had no tolerance at all for the newcomer, handsome or not. 302 couldn't get away fast enough, and soon the Druids were all back together and bedded down for the night.

The stranger, however, stayed nearby. Soon enough, it was U Black's turn to slip away and approach the newcomer. This time when 302 ran off, the eager female was right alongside him. Seconds later 21, joined by 253, came racing through the trees, charging after the black male wolf and the young female. 21 passed U Black and was bearing down on 302, who was running scared—so scared, in fact, that he ran right through a herd of bison and kept on going.

Confident that the problem with the unwelcome intruder was solved, and that he'd seen the last of a wolf that clearly wasn't willing to risk a fight in the name of love, 21 turned and trotted back toward his family. That's when 302 made what appeared to be a stupid, and potentially fatal, mistake. He ran directly at 21, apparently willing—at last—to challenge the Druid alpha male. 21 turned and saw 302 racing toward him. Furious now, 21 instantly ran straight at the newcomer. It was clear he was planning a very unpleasant reception for the stranger.

302 quickly came to that same conclusion, lost his nerve, and decided a hasty retreat might be the best strategy. But he wasn't fast enough. 21 caught up and

A Time of Legends

wasted no time in pinning the younger wolf. The newcomer did not fight back. Instead, he lay on the ground, completely submissive. 21 could have torn the interloper apart, but that had never been his way and he wasn't about to change now. He did not attack, choosing instead to hold 302 down to assert his power; then 21 stepped back and allowed the black male to run off. Once again, 21 returned to his family and led the pack back into the trees—all, that is, except for one. U Black went the other way. She rejoined 302 and, after some tail-wagging and flirting, the two ran off together to the west.

U Black's decision forced 21 to race after the pair and chase off 302 for the fourth time. Later in the day, U Black—a very determined young lady—once again joined up with 302. 21 chased the pair, caught 302, and held him down. 302 immediately went limp and submissive, and 21 released him again. 302 had figured out something important: if he didn't fight back, 21 would let him go, and he could then resume his efforts to lure the Druid females away from their home pack. It was a cowardly strategy, but it worked.

302's unwillingness to fight showed itself again later that same day during another of his advances. This time, he was chased off by one of the Druid yearling males, a much younger and smaller wolf. But the strategy was still working. A couple of days later, 302, all three young adult Druid females, and even the young

An Incredible Journey and a New Arrival

male yearling were together atop a nearby hill. With the sun setting behind them, the five wolves set up a group howl. The following day, the two Druid pups had also joined the renegade group, which now numbered seven.

It wasn't long before the Druid alphas, accompanied by 253, arrived on the scene. After greeting the six Druids that were part of the breakaway group, the adults went after 302. This time it was 42 who got hold of the handsome intruder, and she wasn't nearly as gentle as her mate had been. She got her jaws around 302 and shook him. Hard. When 302 finally broke free and ran off, he was a little more reluctant to return than he had been after his encounters with the endlessly forgiving 21.

Even so, the rebel had not completely given up. 302 eventually returned to the Druid area accompanied by a younger brother, and the two young males continued to spend time with the three Druid young adult females. But even though 302 was handsome and a big hit with the Druid females, he didn't always treat them well—certainly not the same way 21 treated female wolves. This was made very clear on a cold winter morning in early February, when 302, his brother, and U Black were feeding on a recent elk kill. U Black pulled a piece of meat off the carcass and stepped back to feed on it, which is exactly when 302 ran over, pounced on U Black, and took the meat.

Despite the rude behavior, the three Druid females seemed willing to forgive 302 for his wrongdoings and remained infatuated with the bad-boy wolf. And their romantic interest continued into late February. For the next several weeks, they alternated between their Druid family and the company of the two brothers. Eventually, though, the Druid females seemed to tire of 302's act, perhaps deciding that he really didn't measure up as a proper alpha male. One by one they dumped the handsome but disappointing suitor and returned to their former pack—first 255, then U Black, and finally Half Black.

As spring approached, it was clear that the Druid females were all pregnant. 42 had been bred by 21, and all three of the young Druid females by either 302 or his younger brother, 301. At the end of March, 302 was once again hanging around Lamar Valley, but he did not approach the Druid pack. He may have been intimidated by 253, whose front leg was almost completely healed. This meant that the second-in-command male Druid would be a formidable foe for a trespassing 302.

By late April, three of the four Druid females had given birth to litters of pups. 21 would now be raising not only his own pups but those sired by 302, who was now back living with his parents.

A Good Druid Year

It was late spring 2003. Most of the snow had gone and warmer temperatures were moving into the meadows of Yellowstone National Park. An elk had died of natural causes just south of the Druids' den, but a grizzly had found the carcass before the wolves could get to it. The Druids weren't about to let that stop them. As evening fell, alphas 21 and 42, accompanied by 253 and U Black, caught the scent of the elk and went directly to where the carcass lay.

The four hungry wolves surrounded the bear. 21 knew exactly what needed to be done. He leaped in and bit the bear on the behind, not once but twice. As the enraged grizzly chased 21, the other wolves, two of them nursing females, rushed in to feed.

The bear repeatedly charged at 21, trying to swat him with a massive front paw. It was dangerous work: if the bear connected with 21 even once, the blow would

A Time of Legends

Wolf 21 confronts a bear

very likely kill him. But 21 had done this sort of thing before. He expertly dodged this way and that, leaping forward and then back, always just out of the huge grizzly's reach.

The bear became so frustrated with these annoying creatures that he finally sat on top of the carcass, daring the wolves to come close. Once again, the four wolves surrounded the bear and his treasure. The grizzly swatted at 21. Then, as 21 grabbed a piece of meat from one end of the carcass, 253 did the same at the other end. The bear went after one of the male wolves, and then the other—which gave the two females a chance to get to the carcass and feed. Mission accomplished.

A Good Druid Year

Thirteen pups were born to the Druids that year. As had been the case in the past, once the pups got to the age that they could consume meat, 21 carried the bulk of the load when it came to feeding them. On any number of days, the big alpha would arrive with a full belly and a large chunk of elk meat in his mouth. He would then regurgitate for the pups and drop off meat for the females who couldn't abandon the pups to join in the hunt. And the endlessly persistent and annoying (especially for 21) 302 began to show up in Druid territory again. In July he was once again hanging around Lamar Valley, following his pattern of alternating between his home pack (the Leopolds to the west) and the Druids. His fascination with the Druids—despite considerable risk to his own health if 21 or 253 caught up to him—may have been because he knew that some of the pups in the pack were his sons and daughters.

◇ ◇ ◇

There were other challenges for the Druids that year, including having to occasionally battle neighboring wolf groups that trespassed into Druid territory. On the first day of September, the Slough Creek pack ventured toward a big bison carcass that was occupied by the Druid adults—all except 253, who was back at the Chalcedony rendezvous site babysitting some of the pups. Five Slough adults and four pups were heading for the kill, anticipating a meal.

A Time of Legends

One of the Druids spotted the approaching wolves and charged directly at the intruders. The rest of the Druids followed, racing toward the Sloughs, who responded by running full-out at the approaching Druids. Wolf 217—who was the founding alpha female of the Slough Creek pack but had been raised a Druid—ran near the front of the oncoming Sloughs but then veered off before reaching her birth family. The rest of the Sloughs barged into the middle of the nine Druids. As soon as they realized they were seriously outnumbered, they scattered in several directions. There was one fight between rival wolves, but the battle was short-lived. Throughout the skirmish, 21 had remained close to 42. He was guarding his mate, making sure nothing happened to her during the fight.

The Druids gathered, howled, spotted 217—and took off after their former pack member. Though they could have caught and injured or even killed her, they were satisfied just to chase her off. Some of the Druids pursued one adult male, and 21 chased another, this one a big gray. But again the Druids were content to see the intruders running away and did not pursue them further.

That evening the Druid adults brought their pups to the bison carcass, but the pups, never having encountered an animal that big, alive or dead, were reluctant to eat. They would approach and sniff the carcass but then back away. By the next morning, the young ones had overcome their nervousness and were happily dining on bison meat.

At about the same time, 302 returned to Lamar Valley and caught the scent of the bison. He immediately approached the carcass and encountered a Druid female yearling, Wolf 286. She was black, and 302 may have mistaken her for 21 or 253, who were also black, because he quickly ran off. Eventually he returned to the carcass, and when he saw that the black wolf was 286—a wolf he knew—the two of them frolicked for a while before they ran off into the woods together. Clearly, 302 had not lost his ability to charm females.

302 had stamina. He regularly made the 25-mile (40-kilometer) trek from his family's home at Blacktail Plateau—a vast open area with low rolling hills due west of Druid territory and home to his family, the Leopold pack—to Lamar Valley, where he enjoyed friendly visits with the Druid females and checked on the pups he had sired. But he was always careful to avoid 21 and 253.

By October, 302 was traveling with a gray female and two pups that may have been the survivors of a litter that had been born to Wolf 251, a former Druid female who had died in June. The gray female had taken over the raising of the two pups, but she was now much more interested in the handsome 302 and flirted with him every chance she got.

I had guessed that 302 knew young females in packs other than just the Druids, and this unknown female seemed to prove that. I wondered how many females he had romanced during the two mating seasons he had lived through as an adult. Since he seemed to have a short attention span, it was probably a lot. ★ RICK

It was around this time that 253 suffered yet another leg injury, his third, this time on the left front. But as had been the case with both of his previous leg injuries, he didn't let it keep him from his regular duties, including taking his turn leading the Druids when they were on the move. He traveled keeping the injured leg in the air and lay down to lick the sore paw whenever the group stopped. But when they resumed their travels, 253 was up and ready to go.

Meanwhile, 302, the gray female, and the two pups were still together and still in the area, even though the Agate pack, a much larger group, weren't far away. 302 and his small troop were attracted to a fresh elk kill just south of the road that ran through that part of Yellowstone. They went to the carcass and began to feed, although they seemed nervous, sensing that the Agates might be nearby. The two adult wolves kept looking around, perhaps picking up the scent of the other pack, and finally they left. The two pups stayed behind and continued to feed. Then, suddenly, they too turned and ran.

A few minutes later, a desperate, high-pitched bark-howl—the call of a wolf in distress—echoed through the forest. The gray female cautiously returned to the area, but 302, as he had always done, refused to fight, even to defend the pups; he was running as hard as he could away from that place. Sadly, the pups had stayed too long at the carcass and were unable to outrun the Agates. Both pups were killed, which meant that none of Wolf 251's final litter survived.

> **Wolf 302—the acting alpha of this small group and possibly the father of the two pups—had saved himself by running away. The most basic responsibility of a male wolf is to defend his pack. 302 had repeatedly failed in that duty. ★ RICK**

◇ ◇ ◇

It was December and winter had settled firmly into Yellowstone National Park. Breeding season was fast approaching—a time 302 particularly looked forward to. December 15 saw him back in Druid territory, and immediately a familiar pattern played itself out. U Black, Half Black, and 255, the three young Druid females, were excited to see the rebel 302 "back in town." And 21 was kept busy trying to keep 302 away from his daughters. The problem, of course, was that the daughters seemed intent on doing all they could to escape their father's control and ran to 302 every chance they got.

This time, though, there was a new wrinkle. When the Druid adults were away from the denning area, 302 stopped by and visited with the pups, some of which were his. The pups got along well with their handsome, charming father, licking his face and jumping up on him, although, true to form, 302 fled when the adult Druids returned.

This pattern continued until the end of the year, when 302 took a break from the Druid females and returned to his birth family at the Blacktail Plateau area.

> At the end of 2003, there were 174 wolves in fourteen packs throughout the park. That turned out to be the highest population ever for Yellowstone. The original wolf population before wolves were eliminated from the park was around 100. The counts estimated to be around 100 took place when the elk numbers were above what vegetation in the park could support. When the elk population dropped down to a more sustainable level, wolf numbers reverted to the long-term average. ★ RICK

Two Farewells

In January 2004, there were seventeen Druids, including nine pups. Of those nine, five had been sired by 302, meaning that more than half of the pups 21 would be raising that year had been fathered by his no-good nephew.

21 and 42 were just under nine years old and had been together every day for more than six years. They had grown old together, but they were still best friends and cared for one another as much as they always had. On the night of January 31, the pair mated and then bedded down just east of Slough Creek. 21 draped a paw over 42's shoulder as the two drifted off to sleep. It was a peaceful, gentle time.

But during the night, that all changed. The Mollie's, a rival pack intent on taking over at least some of the Druid territory, attacked. While 21 fought with some of the big males, several of the Mollie's were able to separate 42 from her pack. They went after her, chasing her across the Lamar River and up to the high ground of Specimen Ridge, where they caught her. She fought bravely for her life and she fought well, but there were too many enemy wolves and she didn't have time to send out a howl for help. There would be no dramatic rescue this time, no posse of Druids led by 21 racing to her aid. He was far away, fighting to protect the rest of the family. She was alone and she was outnumbered. And finally, she was overcome and fatally wounded.

When the fighting was over and the two sides had stepped back, 21 realized that 42 was missing. He set out to look for her, but he likely lost the scent at the point where she had crossed the river in her flight from her pursuers. He rejoined the main pack and then, with the other Druids, returned to the area where he had lost his mate's scent. But again he was unable to find her. Not then. Not ever. The pair that had been together for so long and had cared for one another as much as any wolf pair ever had would never be together again.

In the small town of Gardiner, just outside the north entrance to Yellowstone, the nonprofit organization Yellowstone Forever has a visitor center and store. Inside the building is an exhibit room with displays about the park. A statue is among the exhibits. That statue could

have depicted any one of the prominent individuals who has played a major role in the history of Yellowstone. But that statue is of none of those worthy candidates. It is a statue of Wolf 42. ★ RICK

◇ ◇ ◇

Despite the devastating loss of 42, life in the pack carried on. For the time being, at least, 302 had moved on, perhaps with the hope of finding companionship that came with fewer complications than the Druid females, who now seemed enamored with males from the Leopold and Mollie's packs. But that didn't mean 21 was able to take it easy. Wolf 376 was a young adult female that was as hard to control as U Black and Half Black had been. The difference was that she wanted to hang out with a large black male from the Mollie's pack. 21, ever the watchful father, was doing all he could to keep the pair apart. And as the case had been with his other daughters, he was largely unsuccessful.

Despite the busyness of chasing off unwanted suitors, 21 was spending more and more time by himself. He was lonely and depressed. Most of all, it seemed like he was missing his longtime mate. 21 had always had a spark—something that made him unique among alpha males. Now, much of that spark was gone.

A troubling thought came to me around this time. For more than six years, 21 had been with 42 every day. She was his priority and he had protected her. Did he feel that he had let her down? What good was it to be the pack's alpha male if he couldn't protect his mate? Of course, we can't know what Wolf 21 was thinking, but it's hard not to imagine that the psychological effect of thinking that he had failed her would have been devastating to a wolf like 21. ★ RICK

◇ ◇ ◇

It was the first day of March. A warm and gentle breeze was coming out of the west across Lamar Valley, and with it came 302 and the gray female with whom he'd had an on-and-off relationship.

A male from the Swan Lake pack who had approached 21's daughters back in January was still hanging around as well. When he saw 302, he tucked his tail between his legs. Surprisingly, 302—the wolf who had always been reluctant to fight or stand up for himself or his family—charged, chasing the Swan Lake male across the road. When 302 returned to the group, one of the pups he had probably sired romped playfully around him. Had 302 been driving away a male that was interested in his daughter? If that were the case, the tables truly had turned: the wolf who had always been the bad boy, the one being run off by the protective father—most often 21—was now the protective father. Maybe things were changing at last for 302.

Back in February, a few weeks after Wolf 42's death, 253 had again left the Druids to set out on his own. His departure had left only two adults in the pack, 21 and Wolf 286, who had taken over the alpha female role. This time, 253 wasn't gone nearly as long as he'd been during his marathon journey. He was back within a few weeks, probably after a search for a female to mate with. 21 was very glad to see him. When 253 approached his father and lifted his sore left front foot, 21 licked the paw. When he stopped licking, 253 encouraged 21 to continue—not once but twice. Both times, 21 obliged his son. Then the younger wolf held up his right foot, the one that had been injured in the coyote trap. 21 licked this foot as well.

When the treatments were over, 21 licked his son's face. Over the course of his lifetime, 21 had often been aware of a member of the pack who was suffering from physical pain or just plain sadness, and he had always spent time with the wolf that was hurting. For all 21's toughness, one of his greatest qualities was his empathy—his ability to be there for members of his family when they needed him.

21's shining example of what it took to be a worthy alpha male had not registered with 302. Despite his actually running off the Swan Lake male, 302 was, most of all, the punk who hung out on the street corner checking out the passing females. He had blown back into Druid country again, this time hanging with a group of pups that seemed to think he was pretty cool—all except for one gray pup who got quite aggressive with the older wolf. 302 responded by nipping the pup but then tucked his tail between his legs and ran away. 302's true personality was once again on display as he fled from the much younger and smaller wolf.

And yet none of 302's weaknesses seemed to matter much to the female wolves that continued to find him irresistible. When 302 took off after his confrontation with the pup, Druid female 376 chased after him. When she caught up to him she started flirting—wagging her tail and generally letting 302 know that, coward or not, he was still her guy.

That same sentiment wasn't shared by 21. As April made its gentle spring presence felt throughout Yellowstone, the feud continued. When 21 saw his nephew trying to feed off a bison carcass, he wasted no time in putting the run on 302 yet again. It seemed that this familiar rivalry would never be resolved.

May brought welcome warmth to Yellowstone and with it litters of growing pups. 21 was hard at work, as he always was at this time of year—first bringing chunks of meat to 286, the alpha female who'd had a litter of pups a few weeks before, and then later regurgitating meat to the pups when they got a little older.

Two Farewells

He was also diligent in keeping 302 away even after breeding season had come and gone. To 302's credit, his wanting to be close to Druid territory may have had something to do with a sincere interest in the pups he had sired. That sentiment cut no ice with 21. On one occasion, he pursued his nephew toward a road and was closing ground when the younger wolf dodged between two vans. When 21 wisely decided against dashing through traffic to get to his foe, 302 managed to escape once more. A few days later, 21 was again in hot pursuit of the irritating playboy wolf. This time 302 jumped into the Lamar River and swam for dear life. 21 leaped into the river after him, but 302 was able to get to the other side and make one more narrow escape from his ever-watchful uncle.

Though June often brings the first pleasant days of early summer, June 2004 was reluctant to do so. Still, the cool days and nights didn't keep the wolves from doing their thing. At the Chalcedony rendezvous site, new snow was on the ground and the temperature was hanging around the freezing mark. A fresh bull elk carcass lay not far away, an indication that the Druids had been busy. But for now, during the evening hours, they were bedded down.

Wolf 376, a young adult female, and two of her pups approached 21. 376 licked his face. Her pups and several other wolves, including 21's daughter 255, came to where 21 was bedded down and wagged their tails at him. The pups began wrestling right next to 21, but the wolf that had loved to play with his pups all his life didn't join in. Instead he watched, enjoying their play as a spectator rather than a participant.

A few minutes later, 255 spotted a bull elk as it passed by not far from the Druids. She began stalking the big elk and was joined by a black male yearling. Two more bull elk joined the first, and the three elk were running hard, with 255 and the yearling close behind. 21 watched the drama unfold but didn't leap up and race off to be part of the chase as he had so many times before.

A gray yearling female also joined the pursuit. 255 closed ground on the biggest bull, nipping at its hind legs. The bull stopped and faced the three wolves—255, who wasn't all that big, and the two yearlings, who were even smaller. When the elk ran again, the wolves tried to get hold of its back legs, but the elk kicked out hard and then ran into the river. Though the elk was exhausted, the three wolves just didn't have the strength to bring it down.

21 had seen the chase and the unsuccessful fight, but he did not leave his spot. As darkness fell, 21 moved off, alone and tired... so tired. It took all his strength, but he was finally able to climb to a familiar place in the mountains high above Lamar Valley, a place that held special meaning for him. He and 42 had been there many times, laying together in that exact spot, watching over their family farther down the hill.

On this night, that place was more special than ever to the wolf that had been the greatest alpha male Yellowstone National Park had ever seen or would ever see again. 21 stood for a moment and, with weary old eyes, took a last look around the shadowy darkness that surrounded the familiar landmarks of his home. Then 21 lay down, lowered his head onto his paws, and, for the last time, went to sleep.

> **Why did 21 make such an arduous journey at the end of his life, when his great strength was rapidly diminishing? I think it was because he didn't know that 42 was dead, only that she was missing. He had not found her during his extensive travels through Druid territory, so perhaps he decided to use his final days to go on a quest, to visit one last spot—the Opal Creek rendezvous site—and look for her there. For wolves, such sites hold meaning, and this was a meeting place. 42 wasn't there, of course, but 21 would have sniffed the lone tree in that meadow and picked up her scent from the many times she and 21 had marked it. The scent would have been old, but it was still hers. At least he had that.**
>
> **Can a wolf feel happiness and joy? I think 21 did at that moment. I imagined him walking to the hilltop, where he had bedded down next to his life partner so many times, and lying down to rest. I would like to think that, as he slowly drifted into sleep, the scent from their tree triggered a picture. If so, then the last thing in 21's mind as he lost consciousness for the final time was an image of 42.**
>
> ★ **RICK**

PART TWO

★

The Rise of 302

Wolf 302

A New Beginning

With the death of 21, the Druids found themselves—for the first time in seven years—in need of a new alpha male. There were two candidates for the job. One was 253, Wolf 21's son, who had overcome repeated injuries to remain the second-ranking male in the Druid pack, behind his father. The other was 302, who had been part of the Leopold pack but was now spending most of his time with the Druids.

302 had proven himself to be a wolf that would do almost anything to avoid a fight and who seemed to have none of the self-sacrificing leadership qualities that great alpha wolves like 21 and his adoptive father, Wolf 8, displayed every day of their lives. In fact, 302's greatest talent seemed to be getting female wolves, including some of 21's daughters, pregnant. To be fair, he had also showed an occasional interest in the pups he had sired.

A Time of Legends

With 21 gone, 302 felt more confident around the Druids, and even brought with him a nephew, Wolf 480. Would there be a confrontation with 253? The question was answered within days of 21's death. The two Leopold wolves were hanging out with some Druids when 253 arrived. Instantly, the Leopold wolves attacked. This was it, then—the test. One of the two adult males, 253 or 302, would have to prove through combat that he was worthy of succeeding 21 as the Druid alpha male.

At first 253 and 302 were the main combatants, but eventually they reached a standoff. When 302's nephew raced to his uncle's aid, the two wolves stood on either side of 253. The Druid male knew exactly what to do: he went on the attack, just as his father had done so many times when it looked like he was outnumbered and in trouble. He lunged at 302 and bit him hard. When the going got rough, 302 usually got going— as fast as he could and with his tail tucked securely between his legs. And this time was no different. With 302 no longer in the mix, 253 turned on 480—but 302's nephew wanted nothing more to do with this tough Druid male, and he too ran away. Other Druids joined 253 in the chase after the young Leopold male. They caught and pinned him to the ground and were biting him at will. 302 ran back toward his nephew and, for a moment, it looked like he might actually try to help. But that wasn't the case. In an astonishing act of self-preservation, 302 joined the Druids in inflicting more damage and pain on 480, biting his own nephew while he was down. Eventually the yearling was able to break free of his attackers and run to safety. But if 302 thought beating up a member of his own family would get him on 253's good side, he was wrong. The tough Druid male charged at 302 again.

The same scene played out one more time: the three wolves in combat, followed by a standoff, then 253 on the attack, and 480 again on the ground with the Druids and his uncle taking turns at biting him. This time, the two Leopold wolves ran off in opposite directions. Eventually, the younger of the two looked over and saw his uncle racing away from the fight. Apparently forgetting the older wolf's role in his beating, he raced to catch up with his turncoat uncle, and the two of them fled together with several Druids in pursuit. Eventually the Druids gave up the chase, and 302 and his nephew continued to run until they were well out of Druid territory.

At least this time 302 had actually been willing to fight for what he wanted—although he did so with what he thought was a two-to-one advantage, and then turned on his own tag-team partner when things became difficult. It was a new low even for a wolf with 302's track record. He was a wolf that challenged the traditional roles of an adult male. The normal path for a young male wolf was to seek out a mate, find an unoccupied territory, and set up a family dynamic, taking on two main tasks: the hunting of prey animals that were much bigger and stronger than he was, and risking his own safety to fight off rival wolves that threatened his mate and pups. 302 was unwilling to take on either of those roles.

Would he—could he—change? The answer to that question could be given only by 302 himself.

◇ ◇ ◇

Wolf 21's son, 253, had fought bravely and well—just as his father had done so many times—and defeating the two Leopold wolves in battle had given him the right to claim the role of alpha male for the dwindling Druid pack. But once 253 was the undisputed alpha, it almost seemed as if he didn't really want the job. Throughout that summer he was seldom in Lamar Valley with the Druids. Part of the reason for his absence was that he was related to all of the Druid females, and wolves avoid breeding with close relatives. He needed to look to other packs to find a female he could mate with and start his own family. That and his habit of traveling apart from the pack kept him away from the Druids that summer.

Finding a mate would not be easy, though. And 253 knew that it would also be difficult to introduce a new female to the other Druid females. They would be unlikely to welcome an outside female to the fold. And if 253 and a new mate left the Druids to establish their own pack, that would open the door for 302 to take over as the Druid alpha male without having to fight for the job. It was a scenario that would certainly appeal to 302.

In early August, with 253 still absent, 302 joined up with the Druids and was friendly with Wolf 286, the alpha female who had inherited the position after 42 had died some months before. But 302 was anything but relaxed. He was unsure if he was really the new male leader of the Druids. What if 253 came back? Would he reclaim the role? Would he want to fight 302 again?

When 253 did return to one of the Druid rendezvous sites on August 26, both 302 and 480 stayed away. They ventured back to the area a few days later only to discover that the site was empty. There was not a Druid wolf to be seen. Uncle and nephew did a lot of howling, hoping to make contact with the pack, but they got no response. A few days later, they managed to join up with one of the Druid adult females, 255, in an area of lush hills and ponds called Little America. But she soon left the two males and rejoined the main Druid pack. Shortly after her return, she was babysitting the four pups that had survived from that year's litter (there had originally been nine) while the other adults were off on a hunt.

A grizzly sow and two cubs wandered into the area. The pups raised their tails and were instantly ready for battle, charging at the three bears. 255 joined in as well, but the bears were already fleeing the scene. It's possible that the bears, with their poor eyesight, mistook the pups for full-grown wolves. Pups being pups, they soon lost interest in the bears, who weren't providing much opportunity for entertainment, and began chasing one another and playing tug-of-war instead—just an average day in the life of a wolf pup.

Two days later, 302 and 480 were back in Druid territory, this time in the company of 286. 286 was amusing herself by catching voles, the small rodents that wolves liked to snack on. She caught one but didn't consume it, choosing instead to toss it high in the air and then go capture it again before it could run off. She tossed the unfortunate vole several times and, finally, when it failed to run off, she tried to push it with her nose to get it going. But this time the vole was dead. 286 picked up the tiny corpse and dropped it in front of 480, who had been watching the action. It seemed like she was daring the young male to try to take it from her, but he ignored the vole and instead got up and went to her, and the two of them romped about. Which is exactly when 302 came along and, ever the opportunist, promptly ate the vole.

But not everything went 302's way that season. As late summer drifted into fall, he stepped into a coyote trap that had been put out by a researcher. It was exactly what had happened to 253 a couple of years before. Two of the coyote researchers went to the area and had to fend off bison that were approaching the trapped wolf. Had the bison gotten to 253 first, they would have trampled and killed him. The researchers risked their own safety to keep the massive bison at bay while Park Service staff, including Rick McIntyre, prepared to free the trapped wolf. As the would-be rescuers came closer, 302 was finally able to yank his paw out of the trap and run off, limping.

> **As hard as it can be to watch wolves suffer, park staff generally does not intervene in events that are occurring naturally (that is, if they are part of normal life for the wolves). In the case of 302 and the bison, however, this situation 302 found himself in was not natural—the trap that had snared his leg had been set by coyote researchers. And so, in this case, we stepped in. ★ RICK**

With 253 having left to seek out an unrelated female, the Druids were busy sorting out who would become the next alpha male. Meanwhile, tensions were brewing in Lamar Valley. A couple of rival packs were becoming a challenge for the Druids, who had resided in that valley since the spring of 1996. The Slough Creek pack was formed in 2002 when Druid Wolf 217 had left the pack to pair off with a Mollie's male. The Mollie's were the descendants of one of the three originating packs, the Crystal Creeks, that had been brought to Yellowstone from Alberta. The Druids had fought the Crystal Creek wolves early on and defeated them, causing the Crystal wolves to leave their home in Lamar Valley and find a new territory 20 miles (32 kilometers) south. Now some of the pack's descendants were once again encroaching on Druid territory, looking to take over Lamar Valley. That fall, there was a fight between the Druid and Slough wolves. At one point, several Druids caught and pinned a young Slough wolf. They bit it several times but then let it go. That seemed to indicate the Druids were willing to work out some sort of peace treaty with the rival pack.

But the Slough Creek pack wasn't the only problem facing the Druids. A pair of large wolves from the Mollie's, 378 and 379, had come into Lamar Valley and were lurking nearby, probably visiting Slough relatives and thinking about trying to deliver a knockout blow to the Druids. In late October, with temperatures falling and winter looming, the brothers attacked the Druids, singling out a sleeping male as their target. That sleeping male was 302. The Druids chased off 378, leaving 302 to do his best against 379. But it wasn't long before 302 gave up and ran away—not exactly the best behavior for a wolf aspiring to be the Druid alpha male. A group of Druids chased off 379 as well, but by then 302 was running hard in the opposite direction.

A New Beginning

The next morning 379 was still hanging around, and 480 challenged the much bigger wolf to a fight. Though he was wounded early in the battle, 480 fought hard and finally drove off the challenger. Unlike his uncle, 480 wasn't afraid to stick around when the going got tough.

302 returned to the Druids two days later, holding his right hind leg in the air and limping on a front leg—both injuries he'd sustained during his fight with 379. As 480 approached 302, he held his tail higher in the air than his older uncle, a sign that he saw himself as the superior male and the new leader of the Druids. When the Druids moved off, 302 followed along, keeping his injured hind leg in the air and stopping frequently to lick first a hind paw, then the sore front one.

When 480 came to him, 302 licked him and wagged his tail from a crouched position, clearly acknowledging that his nephew was his leader. Without question, 302 accepted that he was now in a supporting role.

480 was certainly tough, but he had other leadership qualities too. When a pup was pestering him, nipping at him and grabbing and tugging at his tail, the tired alpha—no doubt wanting to take some time for a rest—did not turn on the annoying pup. He was patient with the little guy, willing to interact and even play. It was another key role of the alphas in the pack, and one that great alpha males, like 21, totally enjoyed.

The Slough Creek pack spent more and more time in Druid territory that fall and early winter. In late December, a group of fifteen Slough wolves gathered in the Chalcedony Creek part of Lamar Valley. Seven Druids watched their approach. One of the seven broke from the group and fled farther away from the Sloughs. That wolf was 302. The other six Druids, led by 480, charged at the trespassers. The Sloughs mounted a counterattack, and the Druids, realizing they were seriously outnumbered, split up and scattered into the woods. It proved to be a good strategy. The Slough wolves soon lost interest, gave up the chase, and began drifting back west toward their own territory.

As the year ended, the Druid pack numbered just nine—seven adults and two pups—both females. 253 had again left the Druids, this time for good, eventually settling in the National Elk Refuge near Jackson, Wyoming, where he established the Flat Creek pack and raised six pups. It was a far cry from three years earlier, when the Druids were the largest pack in all of Yellowstone, numbering thirty-eight. Now they were one of the smallest—and about to get smaller.

A Druid Resurgence

As 2005 began, things had reached rock bottom for Wolf 302. Not only was he subordinate to his younger nephew 480 in the Druid hierarchy, but he also now ranked below a black yearling male. In fact, 302 fought the yearling twice and lost both times.

Fighting was not a skill 302 possessed. Or maybe it was the *desire* to fight that he lacked. However, it would soon be mating season, and as he had proved many times, he was skilled at charming females. Though he was third in the male pecking order within the Druid pack, he was undaunted as mating season drew closer. And this year would be even easier for 302, with neither 21 nor 253 around to put the run on him every time he came near a Druid female.

January 12 marked the tenth anniversary of the Wolf Reintroduction Project at Yellowstone, and just a few days after that a crisis began to loom for the diminished Druid pack. With more of the young males leaving to find mates and establish packs of their own, just seven wolves now made up the Druid family. The Slough Creek wolves were well aware of the decrease in the Druid population. With double the number of their rival pack, the Sloughs began making their move to take over Lamar Valley, which had been Druid territory for so long.

The nine wolves making up the Druid pack no longer included 376, a female who had likely been caught and killed by the Sloughs. But it did include 302, the biggest wolf in the pack—though also the one that would provide the least amount of help in a fight with the Slough Creek wolves. The Sloughs moved into Lamar Valley and hung around the Druids' main denning area for a few days, howling to show their superiority. The Druids wisely left the area to avoid a confrontation that would likely have ended in disaster. After a couple of days, the Sloughs drifted back to their home territory, and the Druids were able to return to the most important part of their geographic empire. It was in this area where generations of Druid pups had been born, and more would be born this year if they could keep the Sloughs out of the valley.

302 was on his game again that breeding season, mating with all of the mature females, though 480 did his best to prevent that from happening. 480 was the male leader and an excellent provider and protector,

but when it came to mating, 302 was by far the Druid females' preferred choice—even by alpha female 286, who had earlier rejected his advances.

Not long after mating season, another Druid wolf, female 375, fell victim to the Sloughs. The Druids had been eating at a bison carcass and were attacked by the Sloughs. When they ran off, 375 became separated from the other Druids and suffered several attacks. Though she was able to escape each time, she had been severely wounded and later bled to death. That left only six members of the once mighty Druid pack, who were also facing what appeared to an escalation of violence in their long-standing rivalry with the Sloughs. The killing of the Druid female by the Slough wolves contrasted with the incident the previous year when the Druids chose to spare the life of a Slough wolf they could have killed.

Not everything was bleak for the Druids that spring. On April 1, the remaining pack members went on an elk hunt and brought down a slow-moving bull. The Druids had worked well together as a team to overcome the elk, and 302 had been a contributing member. And around that same time, the pack also experienced a bright ray of sunshine in a period of cloudy skies—their alpha female used a den site at the far eastern portion of Druid territory, far from where the Slough wolves ranged, to have seven pups. If the Druids had good pup survival, their increased numbers would allow them to better withstand the aggressive behavior of the Sloughs.

As it turned out, the Sloughs were about to encounter a difficulty that had nothing to do with territory or getting along with the neighbors. That spring, four of the Slough females had litters—sixteen pups overall, seven grays and nine blacks. But an outbreak of distemper took the lives of twelve of those pups. Distemper is a canine disease that can be spread to the wolves by pet dogs that visitors bring to the park; it is often fatal to wolves. The outbreak affected some of the other packs as well, but the Sloughs were hardest hit.

While the Sloughs were dealing with severe losses in their pup population, the Druid numbers also continued to dwindle. Of the six pups born to 286 earlier that year, only one survived. In addition, 286 herself as well as adult female 255 both died that summer. That left the Druid pack numbering just five wolves, and that number dropped to four with the death of the last of the pups. Now the pack was made up of 480 and 302 as well as two female yearlings. The Sloughs continued to occupy parts of what had been Druid territory. Though they were small in number, the Druids did make one act of defiance that year: they crossed into the Slough Creek area and took down an elk in enemy territory.

While the pendulum had swung away from the Druids and toward the Sloughs in terms of numbers, it hadn't been so long since the Druids had dominated the region as the largest pack. Perhaps one day the pendulum would swing back.

And, in a way, that's what happened. In 2006, for the second year in a row, the Sloughs suffered through a tragic denning season, although the trouble was of a very different kind from the previous year, when illness had kept their pup survival rate so low. This year, four Slough females were pregnant. They had just settled into their den when a pack of outsiders, known as the Unknown pack, arrived from north of the park. These wolves were trouble. Soon after their arrival, they killed the third-ranked Slough male and a female companion. But that was just the beginning. The Unknown pack, with six adults and six younger wolves, drove off the Slough males and set up camp right next to the den where the Slough females were having their pups—which meant it was very dangerous for those females to come out to feed or get to water. The Slough males were also afraid to come near the den, either to bring the females food or to try to drive off the invaders that had taken over the denning area. The siege went on for weeks. To make matters worse for the entrapped mother wolves and a few young females who were with them, the Slough Creek males eventually abandoned them altogether and even took up with another female. The Unknowns also killed another of the Slough males, leaving only one, and he was not about to risk his life in an attempt to rescue the females.

The marauding Unknown males and females tried repeatedly to enter the den. Each time, though, they were kept at bay by an angry mother wolf who managed to keep the intruders from getting through the narrow opening. Eventually the siege ended, but not before major damage had been done to the once-powerful Slough Creek pack. Two of their three adult males had been killed and, despite the heroic efforts of the mothers who had been under siege in the dens, no pups survived. The Sloughs' number had been reduced to eight. It was a significant development for the Druids. Although they numbered only four, if they had a solid pup survival rate that year, they could soon outnumber the pack that had driven them from their home territory.

That pendulum had, in fact, swung back.

◇ ◇ ◇

The wolf mating season began in the final week of January and lasted through much of February, with the resulting pups born in April. Wolf 480, the Druid alpha male, mated with 529, the new alpha female, while 302 mated with the other Druid female, 569. Soon enough, both females were pregnant. If all went well, a Druid comeback was possible.

There was, however, a potential problem—or, rather, two potential problems. The Unknowns were still in the area, and there was no guarantee that they wouldn't be looking to wreak the same kind of havoc on the Druids that they had on the Sloughs. And, of course, the

A Druid Resurgence

remnants of the Slough pack was also nearby. For the Druids, this meant that the choice of a denning area was critical. They needed to avoid both a confrontation with the Sloughs and having the Unknowns lay siege to their denning area. The Druids chose well, selecting an area called Round Prairie, about 5 miles (8 kilometers) east of their traditional denning site. Two creeks, Pebble and Soda Butte, met there, creating a feeding area for elk, bison, and moose, and thickly forested slopes surrounded all sides. Both Druid females had litters, eleven pups in all with eight of them surviving. 569's litter of seven pups was unique. Because she had mated with both 480 and 302, six of her pups were sired by 480 and one by 302. While this was a bit unusual, given the mating habits of wolves, it is not impossible to have multiple fathers within the same litter.

The Druids were able to make frequent kills in the Round Prairie area. This was good for the two nursing mothers, who required extra nourishment to help them produce milk for their young pups. And later, when the pups moved on from nursing to consuming meat, the plentiful supply of prey animals would again be important.

There is one more thing to mention about the 2006 denning season. Early in April, I saw Agate female 472 and noticed that she looked pregnant. 472 had been born to

the notorious and mean Wolf 40 but had been raised by 42, the kinder, gentler sister. Her father was 21. Although 472's pregnancy did not seem particularly significant at the time, it turned out that one of the tiny embryos she was carrying was of a female pup that would grow up to play a major role in the Yellowstone story. That pup would even become famous around the world, thanks to *She Wolf*, a television documentary made by Bob Landis that aired in 2014. You'll get to read more about that "06 Female" (her name referred to the year of her birth) in the third book in the Chronicles of the Yellowstone Wolves series. ★ RICK

In June 2006, four Unknown wolves were away from the rest of their pack and hanging out at the Druids' Chalcedony rendezvous site. And they were howling. The four Druid adults arrived to investigate the wolves that were trespassing on their territory. Seeing the Unknowns, the Druids immediately attacked, charging straight at the intruders with 480 in the lead. The Unknowns, not nearly so bold when they didn't have all of their packmates around them, ran off. The Druids caught up to one black yearling, pinned him, and bit him several times. They finally let the yearling go and chased the other three. Eventually, all eight wolves met up and fought until the Unknowns lost their nerve and ran away again, with the Druids pursuing and biting at their hindquarters. That battle turned out to be the last gasp for the nasty Unknowns. They left Druid territory for good. And it was the small pack of four Druids that had put the run on the rival pack, something the Sloughs wolves had never done, despite having many more members than the Druids.

With the arrival of summer, the Druid pups were now two months old and able to travel. On a June day under a brilliant blue sky, with the sun sending warmth into Lamar Valley, the two Druid alphas led the family on an excursion. Five of the pups trailed after them, and behind them was 302, dutifully riding herd. He spent a lot of time looking around, as if searching for more pups. And that's exactly what he *was* doing. Because when all of the pack came together later that day, it was clear that there weren't just five new pups in the group. Eleven young Druids had entered the world just ten weeks before—the surviving pups from the two litters. The next day, 302 was on babysitting duty, having gathered all of the pups around him in a nearby meadow. When 302 wandered off into the trees, the pups followed. And he regurgitated meat for the young ones to eat. It was the Wolf 302 Day Care Center. The second-ranking adult male, who hadn't once demonstrated the leadership traits that being an alpha male required, was taking this role seriously. And surprisingly, he was a pretty darn good day care leader.

The year rolled on. It was a peaceful and happy time for the Druids. All eleven pups survived the first six months of their lives, which are always the most

A Time of Legends

difficult and dangerous as they face the possibility of malnutrition, disease, and attacks from rival packs.

There were a couple of incursions from the neighboring Sloughs, but they seemed less willing than usual to take on the Druid pack, especially now that the numbers had swung back in the Druids' favor. A couple of incidents in October demonstrated the changing dynamic. The Slough pack returned to Lamar Valley, but when they encountered the superior force that was now the Druids, they beat a hasty retreat back to their own territory. A few weeks later, once again in Druid territory, the Sloughs took down an elk, but they abandoned the carcass to the Druids when the larger pack arrived from the east and claimed the elk as their own. The Sloughs may not have realized that though the Druids had superior numbers, most of their pack were pups.

December brought heavy snow and extremely cold temperatures, but for the Slough pack, the weather was the least of their concerns. They suffered another crushing blow when their alpha male was killed by other wolves, likely some Unknowns that were still hanging around the area. All of the remaining Sloughs were female, and with breeding season coming and no male for the females to mate with, the situation was dire indeed. Fortunately, a gray yearling from the Agate pack joined the Sloughs. While a wolf his age would no doubt have a difficult job fulfilling all the duties of an alpha male, at least the breeding of the Slough females was no longer an issue.

Although they hadn't faced the same challenges as the Sloughs, the Druids hadn't made it through the year completely unscathed. As 2006 wound down, the pack had lost three of the eleven pups that had been born that spring. Alpha female 529 was also gone from the pack and presumed to have died—cause unknown. That left three adults—alpha male 480, new alpha female 569, and 302, along with the eight surviving pups. 302's situation hadn't changed much. He was still looking after the family's pups and continued to rank below his nephew. More and more, it was looking as if 302 would live out his life as a subordinate male who was popular with the female wolves and pups but who wouldn't accomplish much more than that.

◇ ◇ ◇

302 decided on a different approach to the 2007 mating season. Because he was related to a number of the young Druid females, he opted to try his luck with the females in some of the neighboring packs. One morning, he headed for an area north of Slough Creek. There were no Slough wolves there at that time, but he did find some of the Unknown females and began spending time with them—a dangerous move given that Unknowns had already killed three Slough males. It seemed 302

was a slow learner. He apparently hadn't figured out that the males of a rival pack weren't likely to welcome him with open paws. Either that or his desire to lure females away from their home packs was greater than his desire to be safe.

Sure enough, his plan backfired. A few days later he was back in Druid territory with a badly injured hind leg and other injuries that indicated he'd probably had several unfriendly encounters with male Sloughs or Unknowns and had paid a heavy price for his efforts to mate with females from those packs.

302 may have been back in Druid country, but there were no Druids to be found. The pack seemed to have disappeared. He howled to try to make contact with his packmates, but had no luck. He struggled to get through the deep snow without having to use his hurt leg, but that didn't work either. He often fell through the surface crust of the snow and had to use that leg to push himself out.

It was a difficult and painful time for 302. He found the remnants of an elk carcass, but with nothing much left but the bones, he didn't get much of a meal. He howled again, desperate to find the rest of the Druids, but still received no answer. He worked his way toward the Round Prairie denning area and finally found the rest of the pack. But the reunion was short-lived. When they moved off, he had trouble keeping up and was left

A Druid Resurgence

behind—alone again. 302 had to struggle on by himself until, finally, there was a second reunion a few days later, this time at a carcass site.

Wolf 302 had always behaved somewhat strangely around carcasses. Early in his life, he had been kicked during a battle to bring down an elk, and the encounter clearly made a lasting impression. He seemed not to realize that once the animal was dead, it couldn't hurt him anymore. He was nervous around carcasses and often reluctant to get close enough to feed. When one of the wolves pulled a strip of meat and made the carcass move, 302 would jump back. Often he didn't eat from the carcass at all, preferring to scavenge bits of meat the other wolves dropped as they ate.

As the 2007 pups got a little older, 302 came up with another strategy for getting meat without getting too close to the carcass. He would wait until one of the pups had eaten his fill. Then he'd approach the pup, lick its face to initiate regurgitation, and eat the regurgitated meat. It was the exact opposite of the behavior that normally happens in wolf families, where the adults regurgitate meat for the pups. Sometimes he would also wait for 480 to regurgitate meat for pups or a pregnant female, and then butt in and steal some of that meat.

In addition to his typical selfishness, 302 was also still displaying the cowardliness that had become his trademark when faced with a threat. At the first sign of a challenge from a rival wolf, the handsome black male lit out as quickly as possible. On one occasion he even ran away from the Druids; they were a long way off and he may have mistaken them for some of the Unknowns. Wolf 302 was seven years old now and had lived through plenty of challenges—both to his own health and safety and to that of his pack—but the bad boy of Yellowstone showed no signs of growing up.

> **As I thought about 302, I wondered if he had gone through some kind of traumatic event when young, something that was now shaping his behavior as an adult. I wondered if a big male had come into the Leopold pack when 302 was a pup or yearling and away from his father and the other adults. If that wolf had attacked and severely beaten up 302, I could see how it might have traumatized him for life and made him fearful of being killed in a fight with other wolves. ★ RICK**

The Times, They Are a-Changin'

March 22, 2007, was a critical day. 302 was resting, alone, near an old moose carcass at the northern base of Mount Norris. The Mollie's were nearby, much higher up on the western slope Norris—five adults and five pups. The Druids were about a mile to the west, nine of them—adults 480 and 569, and seven pups. The Mollie's howled and the Druids howled back. And so it began.

480 moved toward the Mollie's with the rest of the Druids right behind him. They crossed the Lamar River and started up the western slope of Mount Norris. It was exactly what 21 would have done in a similar situation, but it was a risky strategy. The only other adult, Wolf 569, was heavily pregnant; she would have trouble running either at the enemy wolves or away from them. The pups, for their part, had never been in a battle and would likely flee if a fight started, leaving 480 to face five Mollie's adults on his own. Before the two sides met

on the battlefield, 569 slipped away—a good decision as she would likely have endangered both herself and her unborn pups if she'd stayed to fight.

The battle started quickly, with four of the Mollie's attacking and pinning one of the Druid pups. 480 charged to the rescue with the other four pups following him. He chased and attacked one of the Mollie's adults, took it down, and then stepped back and let it go. While that was happening, the embattled pup managed to escape its attackers.

A black Mollie's male ran at 480. He immediately countercharged, sending the enemy wolf on a getaway run. 480 and the Druid pups gathered together, looking defiant in the middle of the battlefield. When a Mollie's came at them, 480 ran at it, met up with it, and pulled it down. He let it go and charged again, this time crashing at full speed into the side of another of the Mollie's. Once that wolf was on the ground, 480 again let it go. Several more times, Mollie's started charges at 480, but they always turned and fled when he ran right at them. Finally, the battle was over.

302 had not engaged in the fight. He had, for the most part, recovered from the injuries he'd sustained when trying to visit females from other packs. And he had to have heard the howls between his packmates and the rival Mollie's. Yet he never moved from his spot. He remained hunkered down near the moose carcass and

let the battle go on without him as he fed and napped—yet another indication of his selfishness and failure as a team player.

◇ ◇ ◇

Mother Nature apparently forgot it was spring, and 12 inches (30 centimeters) of snow fell on Yellowstone in early April. But the nasty weather wouldn't stop the natural cycle of life in the wolf packs. That month, Wolf 569, the alpha female Druid, denned up near Cache Creek, a tributary of the Lamar River. Soon afterward, she gave birth to seven pups.

The Sloughs, denning at their traditional spot west of Slough Creek, had a total of thirteen pups that spring. Some had been sired by the young gray wolf that was now their alpha male, and some, very likely, by 302, who had spent time in the area during the mating season and had the injuries to show for it.

Throughout that summer, the Slough alphas and other pack members were making frequent and worrisome forays into Druid territory, making kills in Druid hunting grounds. If that habit continued, a confrontation between the two packs was a certainty. Another gray male had joined the Slough pack and seemed to have been accepted by the alpha, but tragedy was about to strike the Sloughs again. The young alpha male was tracking a bull elk the pack had attacked and hurt earlier in the day. Intent on finding the injured elk, he was struck and killed by a car as he attempted to cross the road running through the park. The newly arrived gray was still with the pack, but if he had any ideas about stepping into the alpha role, they were quickly dismissed. A big black male arrived on the scene and ran off the gray. That black wolf was 590, the brother of the gray that had been killed on the road. 590 had been with the Sloughs previously and was quickly accepted by the pack's females and pups.

Cars and roads were sometimes deadly for the Yellowstone wolves. Many of them were quite rightly afraid of both and avoided them whenever possible. But here again, 302 broke with normal wolf behavior. He was not particularly worried by the traffic that moved through the park, occasionally very close to wolves as they traveled from place to place within the park. In fact, 302 would actually use the road sometimes to save time. And it was this lack of fear—of roads, cars, and the people in those cars—that allowed him to save the day during a late-season hunt.

It was a still, chilly November morning in Lamar Valley, and the Druids were looking for food. Soon they were chasing a herd of elk and had singled out a calf that ran into the river in an attempt to escape. As the calf made for the deeper water, 480 followed.

The calf weighed about 260 pounds (118 kilograms) and turned to face its pursuer. 480 leaped at it, grabbing the upper part of the calf's throat. He held on, his powerful jaws soon causing the calf to collapse into the water. But suddenly, and before he could finish off his prey, 480 let go and ran off. Not far away, tourists traveling through the park had stopped on the road to watch the unfolding drama. Their presence spooked 480.

That's when 302 swung into action. Unfazed by the activity on the nearby road, he leaped into the water and got hold of the calf in almost exactly the same way as 480 had done. Soon the calf was dead. It would provide welcome meals for the Druids. 302 had let his family and packmates down time after time. But not today. On this day, he was the superhero who got the job done.

The very next day the Druids were once again hunting, and this time they were chasing a group of bull elk. Healthy elk can outrun wolves, but one of these bulls, though he weighed close to 700 pounds (318 kilograms), was not healthy, and the Druids were soon alongside him. The two big males, 302 and 480, worked together, one leaping up and taking hold of the elk's shoulder and the other grabbing the animal's throat. The rest of the wolves bit the elk in different spots, and it was quickly taken down and finished off.

On back-to-back days, 302 had pulled his weight and contributed to the job that needed to be done. At the same time, he'd shown that his fear of big prey animals was a thing of the past. 302 was now seven and a half years old, almost twice the life span of the average Yellowstone wolf. Were these signs, at last, that he was beginning to change his ways? Was he finally ready to become more like some of the outstanding male wolves who had roamed Yellowstone before him—like his uncle, Wolf 21? As he entered his senior years, was Wolf 302 truly reforming and becoming something he had never been in his entire life, or was this change just temporary? Only time would tell.

◇ ◇ ◇

The ongoing feud between the Druids and the Sloughs continued into the fall of that year. The deadly nature of that feud was on full display during one incident that began when the Sloughs, eighteen strong, gathered at a bull elk carcass on the western edge of Druid territory. The Druids, fifteen in number, picked up the scent of the kill and headed in that direction. Both groups had a large number of pups. The Sloughs moved away from the carcass, but one young female remained behind. When she looked up and saw the Druids coming at a dead run, she raced off. The Druids spotted a nearby black Slough pup and focused their attention on it. They soon caught the pup in a hollow and took it down. The Druids came out of the hollow a few minutes later, but the black Slough pup did not. It had lost its life in the attack, which was likely in part retaliation for the earlier death of a female Druid at the hands of the Sloughs. Prior to that, the Druids had never killed a Slough wolf.

Other Slough pups had been separated from the main pack during the fight, and Slough female 380 came back to gather them and move them to safety. She was traveling alone and was putting herself in danger to rescue the pups. The pups howled when they saw her, which was the last thing 380 wanted. She was hoping not to let the Druids know she was in the area, but the pups had blown her cover. Luckily for 380 and the pups, the Druids had bedded down. This time, at least, the Sloughs were able to make their way to safety.

That particular battle may have been over, but the rivalry carried on. On a chilly mid-November day, all sixteen Druids were traveling west through Lamar Valley. With 302 in the lead, they picked up the scent of the Slough pack. Almost immediately, they spotted a black Slough wolf. The pack charged downhill with the younger Druids leading and 302 now at the rear. The black wolf was a young Slough female with an injured leg that was hampering her as she tried to keep up with the rest of her pack. The Druids quickly overtook her, and the result was both fast and deadly. The young Slough female had no chance; within a few seconds, she was dead. This was a second case of the Druids killing a Slough wolf in apparent retaliation for the Sloughs' killing of Druid female 375.

A Time of Legends

As the Sloughs traveled away from the Druids, 302 stood tall on the hillside and watched them go. He had been an active participant both in the campaign to drive the Sloughs away and in the revenge killing of the Slough pup. He seemed to be relishing his role. He was a different wolf from the vagabond playboy who had snacked and napped while the Mount Norris battle was raging nearby. Now, he was helping with the pups. He was an important player in the hunts that provided food the pack needed. And his longtime aversion to fighting appeared to be a thing of the past. He was doing almost all of the traditional jobs of an adult male wolf.

302 continued to watch the Sloughs as they disappeared to the west, with the sun setting before them. Then he turned his face to the sky and howled. The rest of the Druids followed his lead and joined in.

◇ ◇ ◇

As the feud between the Sloughs and the Druids continued, a couple of newcomer males moved into the area. The first was a young, light gray wolf that did a lot of howling, probably because he was looking for a mate. It wasn't long before a young gray Druid female met up with the newcomer and offered a friendly greeting, but the rest of the Druids showed up and quickly drove the young male away.

The second new arrival was also gray but had a darker coat. Almost right away he connected with another of the Druid females, the gray yearling 569. Her mother came along and discouraged the stranger, and then 480 and the rest of the Druids ran the dark gray male off. But he didn't go far.

The arrival of the two males was a sign of events to come. All six of the remaining yearlings in the pack were female. With mating season right around the corner, the two gray males who were hanging around Lamar Valley were no doubt interested in getting together with those females. Perhaps they might even convince them to leave their home pack and run off to start a new one elsewhere. 302's decision to stay with the Druids rather than form a new pack was not typical behavior for older male wolves.

302 had been many things in his life—not all of them good. For most of his life, he'd put his own needs and self-preservation above everything else, even if it meant abandoning females and pups to what might have been an unpleasant fate. But despite his numerous faults, 302 had always been smart. To be able to have as many liaisons with female wolves as he did—usually with angry fathers and other pack members lurking nearby, eager to teach him a lesson—and come away with as few battle scars as he did was proof of his intelligence. Oftentimes it was a sneaky intelligence, but that didn't matter. 302 was one savvy wolf—and he knew it.

He showed just how smart he was as December rolled along with its deep snow and cold temperatures.

One day, he spotted a group of ravens in some distant trees. As he watched, the ravens would drop toward the ground, stay there a while, and then fly back up into the trees. Although 302 couldn't see what on the ground was so interesting to those ravens, he had a pretty good idea.

He gathered the rest of the Druids and led them to where all the raven activity was happening. Sure enough, when they got there, a bull bison lay dead in the snow-covered terrain. The Druids fed on that carcass for several days, largely thanks to 302's curiosity and intelligence.

A few days later he was once again demonstrating his newfound leadership traits. Assisted by yearling female 571, 302 leaped up and grabbed the throat of a big bull elk. As other Druids raced in to help, 302 wrestled the bull to the ground. There wasn't much doubt about it now: 302 was turning his life around and becoming a major force in the daily life of the Druid pack.

> **Not only was Wolf 302 evolving—he was becoming famous. In 2007 he was featured in a television documentary by Bob Landis. *In the Valley of the Wolves* was shown across the United States on the PBS network. It was such a hit that Landis was asked to do a follow-up. In 2010 *The Rise of Black Wolf* aired around the world on the National Geographic channel. Suddenly, 302 was an international television star! His good looks and bad-boy**

reputation probably played a large part in his immense popularity. Not bad for a wolf that had once looked like he wouldn't be much more than a source of irritation to a whole lot of other wolves. ★ RICK

As the year wound down, the light gray wolf that had recently appeared on the scene was spending time with three of the young Druid females. On one snowy, cold morning, they were together, as both 302 and 480 looked on with distinct wolf disapproval. The gray male crouched with his tail tucked and the two males charged. Light Gray took off and the two Druid males stopped, satisfied that he was fleeing.

But like 302 in his younger days, Light Gray was slow to take a hint. He returned not long after, and this time it was 302 who gave chase. When the younger wolf got mired in the deep snow, 302 threw him down but then slipped in the snow himself. Light Gray got back up, and the two fought on until the younger wolf tried again to run away. Once again 302 caught, pinned, and bit him as he'd done before. The gray wolf fought back and bit 302 hard on the face. When the other Druids ran in, the intruder ran off and the fight ended, but not before both wolves were injured.

Light Gray bedded down away from the Druids and licked an injured front leg, but he had bloody wounds on his side and both hind legs as well. 302's fur was sticking out in every direction and he was walking stiffly, as if he were sore. He wiped a paw over his bloodied face, where Light Gray had bitten him. When he lay down in the snow, one of the Druid females came to him and licked his face to help clean his wounds. 302 licked a front leg, then a back leg. There was a lot of blood in the snow around him.

302, for so long a cowardly non-fighter, had fought well and bravely, solidifying his position as a vital member of the pack.

> The battle with Light Gray was the first time I had seen 302 refuse to give up when fighting another male, even when on the receiving end of what had to be a painful bite to the face. The wolf continued to surprise us with how he was changing. 302 had known three greatly accomplished alpha males in his long life: his father, Wolf 2; his uncle, Wolf 21; his cousin, Wolf 253; and now his nephew, Wolf 480. They were all aspirational role models for how proper alphas should behave, and it looked like 302 was finally beginning to emulate them.
>
> Can a tiger change its stripes? Can a person or a wolf change their basic character in their later years? Against all my expectations, it looked like 302 was doing just that.
> ★ RICK

The New and Improved 302

As 2008 began, there were sixteen wolves in the Druid pack: three adults (480, 569, and 302) along with six female yearlings and seven pups. Mating season was once again approaching and with it came challenges and behaviors unique to that time of year. It wasn't unusual for 480 to pin 302, presumably to remind his uncle that he, 480, was the alpha and would therefore take care of the breeding of 569, the alpha female.

Because 302 was related to most if not all of the female yearlings, the big black wolf realized he was again going to have to look elsewhere if he wanted to mate. 302 was now the same age Wolf 21 had been when 21 made it his ongoing job to try to prevent bad-boy 302 from mating with the young Druid females when he'd first arrived on the scene.

Now the role had been reversed. In addition to trying to figure out his own mating concerns, 302 was spending a fair amount of his time trying to repel the advances of Light Gray and Dark Gray toward the young Druid females. And he was taking the job seriously, as his fight with Light Gray had shown.

As mating season went on, 302 changed his thinking about Dark Gray. He began to tolerate, even befriend the young wolf. Since he could not breed the young Druid females himself, it looked like he at least wanted some say into which wolf did. And Dark Gray had been working hard at being submissive to 302, keeping his tail tucked when the two were together, and even licking 302's face to show that he posed no threat to the higher-ranking wolf.

During that mating season, Light Gray bred at least two of the Druid females, and Dark Gray bred at least three. One of the females had mated with both of the grays.

> **I later told a group of people in Lamar Valley about how the six Druid sisters had to share two boyfriends that year. An eight-year-old girl said "That's never good." ★ RICK**

By the end of the mating season, 302 had gone into Slough, Agate, and Leopold territories in search of female companionship. It was dangerous for a lone wolf to try to lure female wolves away from rival packs, but 302 had done it, successfully, many times. And he was successful again—at least some of the time—during this mating season.

In April of that year, Light Gray was hanging out near the Druid den area. On one cold morning, growls and howls filled the air as Light Gray, in the company of three of the Druid females and four pups, came up against the Druid alpha male. Wolf 480 was not happy, and he attacked the male he had chased off so many times before. This time, though, was more serious. 480's intention wasn't to chase the young male away or pin him down and put a scare into him. He saw the outsider as an invader trying to take over his pack's den site, and that was something he couldn't tolerate.

Light Gray wasn't trying to be a bad guy. He was just acting on a normal wolf instinct, wanting to be near the females he had mated with and the pups he had sired. None of those females had demonstrated a desire to leave their home pack, which meant Light Gray had to risk a dangerous encounter with 480 to be with them. And another factor was at play: Light Gray was losing some of his fur due to a condition called mange. Mange is very contagious and spreads quickly within the wolf population if one or more wolves in a pack become infected. 480 may have picked up an abnormal scent from Light Gray and sensed that the young wolf could be a threat to his own pack. His attack on Light Gray was fierce and, as it turned out, deadly. Perhaps sensing that staying too close to the Druids could have similar consequences for him, Dark Gray kept his distance from the pack.

A Time of Legends

Wolf 302 chases off Light Gray and Dark Gray

Mange is caused by infestations of parasitic mites just below the skin. When a dog or wolf scratches at the spot, the scratching pulls out fur along with the mites. Mange does not kill a wolf outright, but the infestation weakens the animal, and the loss of fur greatly reduces its ability to cope with extremely cold weather. ★ RICK

All six of the young Druid females and the alpha female were pregnant heading into denning season and what promised to be a very busy time for the Druids.

The Slough wolves continued to hunt in Druid territory in Lamar Valley, and that was a complication. 302 knew the Sloughs were nearby and that he'd have to be careful not to be caught by them. Despite his caution, he had a close call when eleven Slough wolves were gathered on a rise close to where 302 and some other Druids had congregated well below that ridge. Though they couldn't see the Druids, the Sloughs raced along the rise, tails raised as they followed the scent of their sworn enemies. Then they charged down the hill to where they thought the Druids had to be. But when they reached the lower elevation, every wolf in the area was a Slough. Moments later, 302 stood on the ridge the Sloughs had just left. He headed east, trotting easily and calmly, convinced he had outsmarted the Sloughs. And he had.

> As the 2008 wolf mating season ended, I thought a lot about 302. He was now nearly eight years old and had lived almost three times as long as the average Yellowstone wolf. Next year he would be the same age that 21 was when he died. If 302 was ever going to take on the risk and responsibility of starting his own pack, he would have to do it soon or he would run out of time. I never told anyone, but I was secretly hoping that he'd end up as the alpha male of his own pack. What a story that would be! ★ RICK

A Time of Legends

◇ ◇ ◇

That summer saw a higher than usual rainfall, and the Lamar River flooded. One day, when the rain had finally stopped but the water remained high, three elk calves were stranded on an island not far from the Druid denning area. The mother elk were able to get to the island to let the calves nurse, so the young ones were fine, but they couldn't or wouldn't leave the island. It was evening and the shadows of darkness were beginning to fall throughout the park.

That's when 302 spotted the calves. He approached the river and was deciding on a strategy to get to the calves when the three mothers charged at him. They cornered him at the top of the steep bank and trampled and stomped on him. Finally, he managed to squirm away, only to have the three adult elk corner and trampled him for a second time. Again he was able to wriggle free, and this time he managed to escape. But the damage had already been done. 302 worked his way deep into a thickly forested area and lay down. Two days passed before he was able to bounce back from the beating he'd taken.

Having failed to get to the three stranded calves, 302's next plan was to steal a carcass from a grizzly he'd spied not far from where he'd been lying low and recovering. He and two Druid yearlings carefully worked their way close to the bear; then 302 and one of the

The New and Improved 302

yearlings dashed in. Each grabbed one end of the calf's carcass and raced away, carrying their prize jointly as they ran. The bear gave chase, and the two wolves had to drop the calf. The bear regained the carcass, but 302 wasn't about to give up. This time, he approached the bear by himself, and when the bear went after him, the two yearlings raced in, grabbed good-sized chunks of meat, and made their escape.

Once they were safely away from the grizzly, the yearlings settled down to dine on the stolen meat. 302 approached but then walked away and let the young wolves have it all. After the bear left, 302 checked out the area and found a calf leg to feed on. He had been willing to take a risk to get food for his young packmates, and he'd followed that up by treating the lower members of the pack with respect. It was yet another example of a wolf whose personality was transforming.

Wolf 302 watches until the pups cross the road safely

10

The Blacktail Pack

The Druid pack's main hunting area was south of the road running through that part of Yellowstone, and their den was north of the road. This meant that the road played an important role in the lives of the Druids, and several other packs as well. Over the years a number of fatalities had occurred on the roads of Yellowstone, as wolves were struck by vehicles.

302 was one of the smartest wolves when it came to dealing with the road. Earlier in 2008, he had shown his traffic awareness: When he was coming toward the road from the south, a car approached and 302 moved to another section of the road. After the car had passed, he got up on the edge of the pavement, looked both ways, and then crossed to the north and headed off toward the main Druid den. Not many wolves understood the concept of cars moving in both directions on a road, but 302 did.

Almost as big a hazard as the vehicles themselves were the people in those vehicles who stopped to watch the wolves. Though it wasn't intentional, their actions sometimes got in the way of the wolves' natural travel patterns.

On one particularly hot summer day, four cars were stopped on the road to watch the wolves. 302 and 569 were on the south side of the road, wanting to cross but unable to with the vehicles in their way. Park staff had to be called out to get the four cars and their occupants to move along. Later that same day, one adult Druid and three gray pups crossed the road to the south. Two of the pups panicked and ran back to the opposite side of the road. Passing motorists spotted the wolves and stopped to observe them. Again, park rangers had to take charge of the situation and have the cars move on. Once the vehicles were out of the way, the wolves were reunited and the crisis was over.

A few days after that, 302, 569, and two black adults crossed the same road. They were heading south with twelve pups trailing along behind them. The pups were different sizes—small, medium, and large—meaning that they came from different litters and were different ages. The adults crossed the creek to the south of the road, but the pups hesitated when they got to the water. Some turned around and looked like they were wanting to run back across the road.

The Blacktail Pack

One brave pup made it across the creek. Another got halfway across but turned back. Two more eventually crossed. Now, three pups and adults were on one side of the creek and the rest of the pups were on the other side, with no desire to set foot in the water. That's when 302 reappeared. Seeing the crisis, he immediately took charge. He swam back across the creek to the pups that hadn't yet crossed. He figured an important first step would be to get those pups back across to the north side of the road. Using his well-developed road-crossing skills, he led the group safely across.

As 302 led the pups in the direction of the den, he stopped several times, looked back, and howled. He seemed to be worried that the three pups who'd managed to get across the creek might get hung up between the water and the road on their way back and not be able or willing to return to the main group. Encouraged by 302's calls, the pups that had successfully crossed the creek were able to come across the creek again, and then across the road. Eventually all of the pups were back together, thanks to the good work of 302—who certainly donned the hero's cloak on that day.

◇ ◇ ◇

In mid-August, 302 and three other Druids discovered a dead bison near the Chalcedony rendezvous site and fed on it. When the four wolves returned to the rest of the pack and regurgitated meat to the pups, it tipped off the other Druid adults that there was a new carcass nearby. It wasn't long before twenty-seven Druids were gathered at the carcass. After feeding on the bison, 569 caught herself a plump squirrel and one of the pups raced over, begging for the treat. But 569 wasn't in a sharing mood, and she polished off the squirrel herself.

While the squirrel mini-drama was playing out, a group of seven Slough wolves were making their way toward the bison carcass. Noting the number of Druids already there, the Sloughs turned back and ran to the west, away from the much larger pack. The days of the Slough wolves bullying the Druids were long gone.

The next morning, a mother grizzly and one of her cubs approached the area where the Druids were feeding. 302 positioned himself between the pups and the bears. When the female grizzly saw the big wolf, she veered off and led her cub away. 302 followed after the bears and was joined by some of the other Druids. One of the Druids bit the cub on the backside, and that sped up the bears' retreat. When they were gone, the Druids gathered round and jumped up and down like they were the Kansas City Chiefs celebrating after a touchdown. The pups had stayed close to 302 throughout the encounter, and they had taken to bedding down near him as well, an indication that they felt secure in his presence. Though 302 wasn't the alpha male, he was

The Blacktail Pack

becoming more and more vital to the well-being of the entire pack. It seemed that 302 had finally grown up.

> **The relationship between 480 and 302 reminded me of the partnership I'd witnessed between 21 and his son, 253. Like 253, 302 was now contributing a lot to the pack, which made it easier for 480 to fulfill his alpha male responsibilities of feeding and protecting his family as well as raising the pups. ★ RICK**

A few days later a quiet evening was interrupted when a grizzly sow and her two cubs came into the rendezvous site to feed on the bison carcass. Several of the young adult Druids charged the bears, and the grizzly family turned and ran. One of the cubs panicked, became disoriented, and was separated from its mother and the other cub. Soon enough, the wolves caught up to it and nipped it, but the cub fought back hard and broke away.

It didn't get far. A wolf came alongside the cub and bit it again. The cub got up on its hind legs and faced the wolf. More Druids rushed in to help, but the bear managed to reach a nearby aspen tree and climbed partway up. One of the wolves jumped up and pulled it out of the tree. The cub escaped again, climbed the tree a second time, and this time fell out of the tree from about 10 feet (3 meters) off the ground. Again the cub squirmed loose from several wolves that were nipping at it, scooted up the tree one more time, and again fell to the ground. But by now, mother and the other cub had come back for the straggler and the three of them marched off, relatively unscathed. It had been mostly a game for the Druids. Had they been more serious about wanting to kill the cub, things might have turned out much differently.

While the game of catch-and-escape was playing out, 302 and another grizzly were both heading for the bison carcass, about 20 yards (18 meters) apart. 302 got to the carcass first and started to feed. Two huge bison bulls were approaching from the opposite direction, but 302 ignored them. The bulls went for the biggest target, the bear, and it quickly left the area. The bulls then turned their attention to 302, who managed to gulp down a couple more mouthfuls before slipping away—just in time to avoid being gored or trampled by the mammoth bison. He had read the situation perfectly, figuring the bison would go after the bear first, and was able to get in a pretty good meal before it became necessary to get the heck out of there.

◇ ◇ ◇

September came to Yellowstone. Leaves were turning yellow, the temperature was dropping, and the ground squirrels had disappeared underground to begin their hibernation—all signs that winter wasn't far off. One day, 302, two younger Druid adults, and seven pups were hanging out at the rendezvous site. Well to the west, the alpha pair and nine adults were also gathered. And a little farther west, the Sloughs were trespassing into Druid territory as they chased a cow elk into the Lamar River.

It wasn't long before the main Druid band spotted the Sloughs and ran directly at them. When the Sloughs scattered, one black wolf ran into the river near the elk. The Druids followed her into the water, caught her, and proceeded to attack. While some of the Druids stayed at the river and continued to bite the black Slough wolf at will, female alpha 569 and the others in the group caught sight of another Slough and went after it.

Off to the west, nine of the Sloughs regrouped and began to howl—a mistake, as it gave away their location. The Druids went after them again, but this time as the Sloughs fled the area, the Druids let them go. The news was not nearly as good for the black Slough female who had been attacked in the river. She had tempted fate many times by trespassing into Druid lands and had finally paid for her brazen—and somewhat foolish—behavior with her life. This was now the third time the Druids had retaliated against the Slough wolves for killing one of their own.

In contrast, around that time Druid alpha male 480 caught a pup that belonged to the small Silver pack, a family that had never bothered the Druid wolves. 480 nipped the pup a few times and then let it go. Later, the Silver alpha male found a Druid pup away from her pack and— just like 480 had done to the Silver pup—let the Druid pup go back to her family unharmed.

Despite the loss of one of their own, the Sloughs were not quite willing to give up. They tried a few more times that day to move into Druid territory, with no luck. Finally, it was the Druid pack, with its superior numbers, who traveled into the Slough home area. They were led by the alphas and 302, and the Sloughs wisely stayed clear of them.

Most of the Druids returned to Lamar Valley the next day, but five yearling males remained behind with 302. By late October it was clear that those five yearlings and a black female Agate had become a subgroup of the Druids—and that 302 was their leader. The subgroup briefly returned to the Druid main pack, and the Agate female rejoined her pack as well, but not for long. Soon the five yearlings and 302 were again traveling west, with no resistance from other packs in the area.

The behavior of this group was unusual. Normally, young males will move off from their home packs one by one, seeking out one or more females in an effort to stake out a territory of their own. But this group seemed to want to stay together, and in mid-November, 302 and his companions were once again on the move. Soon five

Agate females joined 302 and his five nephews. One of those females was Wolf 06, who was now two and a half years old. She was beaten up and bloodied, the result of a confrontation with her aggressive sister, Wolf 693.

Had the confrontation been over 302? No one knows, but one thing became clear when 693 and 302 began double scent-marking—lifting one of their hind legs and urinating on rocks, trees, and bushes to let other wolves know that they were the alpha pair—in an area west of Hellroaring Creek. This was the alpha pair in this new group. It was official. Now an old wolf, 302 had at last established his own pack. His behavior had certainly changed over the last couple of years, but an important question remained: Would he be able to fulfill the heavy responsibilities of an alpha male, or would he revert to his former far-from-heroic behavior and let his pack members down?

The new pack needed a name. At first, the park staff came up with Dragates—a combination of Druid and Agate. But as the year came to an end, and with mating season right around the corner, the pack was bedded down in the Blacktail Plateau area, the territory formerly occupied by the Leopold wolves. 302 had been born a Leopold, so he was both familiar with and comfortable in that area. The Leopolds had fallen apart in recent years, which meant the territory was vacant. The new group was claiming it as their own, and it was only right that they have an official name to go with their new status. They soon became known as the Blacktail pack. Wolf 302—the once irresponsible son of the Leopold alpha male—had come back home and brought his new pack with him. Just like his father before him, he had finally earned the title "alpha."

◇ ◇ ◇

Wolf 06 had been one of the new Blacktails, but though she and 302 got along well, she didn't stay with the pack. The 06 female was already showing signs of the independence and strength that would make her one of the most memorable female wolves ever to roam the woodlands and meadows of Yellowstone. She mated with five males that season but did not get pregnant. She spent some time with the Blacktail and Agate packs, but she preferred to be a lone wolf, probably to escape the abuse from other female wolves, especially her alpha sister 693. 06 was well suited to life as a loner. She was a fierce and accomplished hunter, capable of taking down prey all by herself, without any help from male wolves. She could confront an elk face-to-face, dodge the deadly hooves and charges, and then leap up and grab the much bigger animal by its throat, maintaining an iron grip until the elk collapsed and died.

As the 2009 denning season approached, other changes were occurring in the Blacktail pack. There

The Blacktail Pack

were four males now, including 302, and two females, 693 and 642. In April, Wolf 692, who had been dividing her time between the Agate and Blacktail packs, returned to the Blacktails. 302 was aware of his role as an alpha male and was already working to ensure the well-being of his pack. This included making sure the pregnant females were getting the food they needed to remain healthy as the time for having pups drew closer. On one late March evening, with the sun dropping in the western sky, 302 and the other Blacktails were bedded down in a pleasant meadow near the Blacktail Plateau. After a while, 302 stood up, picked up a big piece of meat he had hidden under his chest, and gave it to 642, who was just a few weeks away from having her pups. It was exactly the kind of gesture Wolf 8 and Wolf 21 had so often made.

That spring both 642 and 693 had a litter, the first-ever crop of Blacktail pups—six in all. 302 was acting just like a father wolf should: he stood guard over the pups and fed them by making many round trips from carcasses, giving meat to both the pups and the mother wolves.

On a dull day in late June, 302 was walking around the denning area. His once-black coat was now turning gray, a sign of his age. Nine years ago, he'd played as a pup on this very same ground. In fact, some of his pups had been born in the same den where he'd been born.

And now here he was, fulfilling the same duties his own father, Wolf 2, had done. He bedded down on a nearby hill, watching over his family.

Two of the young males were near the den as 693 brought an elk antler to the denning area for the pups to play with. A black pup was stalking something not far from a clump of trees. 302 stood up to monitor the pup's movements, making sure he was safe. When 302 was certain all was well, he bedded down again, this time in a marsh the Blacktail adults used as a napping spot in hot weather. Not long after, mother wolf 642 walked over to where 302 lay resting and then set out on a search for several of the pups that were nowhere to be seen. She howled from time to time, but there was no answer from the pups.

302 finally stood up, stretched, and headed north. It took some time, but he eventually found the pups. As soon as they saw him, the pups rushed at him, jumping up and licking his face. 302 tolerated their enthusiastic greeting, and then led them back to the denning site. When everyone was back, safe and accounted for, he regurgitated some meat for them. Then he set off once again for the marsh, the pups following him in single file. The alpha male checked over his shoulder periodically to make sure everyone was still with him. When he got back to the marsh, he lay down again, ready to resume the rest time that had been interrupted by the search for the pups.

But first he watched the pups intently as they played in an area he too had played in when he was a much younger wolf. Three pups tried to sneak up on him. He heard them and turned his head. The pups wagged their tails at him and then trotted away, leaving the old wolf to enjoy a restful nap.

Wolf 302, alpha male and leader of the Blacktail pack, had earned it.

> As I thought about the sequence of events that played out on that June day, I was very impressed by 302. The mother wolf was frantically trying to find the pups but had failed to get answers to her howls, and couldn't find their scent trail either. When she ran off in the wrong direction, 302 sacrificed his nap time and went directly to them—almost as if he knew where they were all along—and then led them back to the rendezvous site.
>
> When he was a pup in this area, 302 would have known all the places he and the other pups liked to explore. He probably never forgot those sites. When he saw 642 trying to find the pups, he got up, apparently made a good guess as to where the pups would be, found them, and brought them back to the denning area. He made it look easy.
>
> Wolf 302 had changed as he neared the end of his life. He had become a wolf like his father, Wolf 2; like his uncle, Wolf 21; and like his nephew, Wolf 480. Being exposed to the behavior and role modeling of those accomplished males showed 302 how a grown-up male wolf should act when faced with difficult and dangerous situations. It took

A Time of Legends

some time, but in the end, he impressed us all by stepping up to the challenge. The wolf that had been a renegade had at last become a hero. And now, as the alpha male of his own pack, the Blacktails, he was not only one of the most famous of the Yellowstone wolves but also one of the greatest. ★ **RICK**

About the Authors

RICK MCINTYRE has spent more time observing and documenting wolves in the wild than any other person. A retired National Park Service ranger and wolf researcher, Rick has watched wolves in America's national parks for forty-five years, twenty-nine of those in Yellowstone, where he has accumulated over 100,000 wolf sightings, worked on the Yellowstone Wolf Reintroduction Project, and educated the public about the park's wolves, including by writing several books for adult readers (*The Rise of Wolf 8*, *The Reign of Wolf 21*, *The Redemption of Wolf 302*, and *The Alpha Female Wolf*). He lives in Silver Gate, Montana. To learn more about him and his books, visit rickmcintyrebooks.com.